The Question Inside of Me

An Adopted Daughter's Quest for Connection

June D. Hawkins-Purifoy

*Priority*ONE
publications
Detroit, Michigan USA

The Question Inside of Me:
An Adopted Daughter's Quest for Connection
Copyright © 2017, 2019 June D. Hawkins-Purifoy

All Scripture quotations, unless otherwise indicated, are from the King James Version.

Scripture quotations marked (NIV) are taken from the Holy Bible, New International Version®, NIV®. Copyright © 1973, 1978, 1984, 2011 by Biblica, Inc.™ Used by permission of Zondervan. All rights reserved worldwide. www.zondervan.com The "NIV" and "New International Version" are trademarks registered in the United States Patent and Trademark Office by Biblica, Inc.™

Scripture quotations marked (NLT) are taken from the Holy Bible, New Living Translation, copyright ©1996, 2004, 2007, 2013, 2015 by Tyndale House Foundation. Used by permission of Tyndale House Publishers, Inc., Carol Stream, Illinois 60188. All rights reserved.

All rights reserved. No part of this publication may be reproduced, stored in a retrieval system, or transmitted in any form or by any means – electronic, mechanical, photocopy, recording, or any other – except for brief quotations in printed reviews, without the prior permission of the publisher.

*Priority*ONE Publications
P. O. Box 361332 | Grosse Pointe, MI 48236
E-mail: info@priorityonebooks.com
URL: http://www.priorityonebooks.com

PAPERBACK
ISBN 13:   978-1-933972-55-8
ISBN 10:   1-933972-55-6

HARD COVER
ISBN 13:   978-1-933972-47-3
ISBN 10:   1-933972-47-5

Editing, Cover and Interior design by PriorityONE Publications

Printed in the United States of America

Endorsements

The Question Inside of Me An Adopted Daughter's Quest for Connection is a must-read book for anyone who has ever felt abandoned, discarded and alone with an insatiable desire to find true connection and a feeling of completion. In this book, June tells her story of being adopted by loving parents as an infant to the reality of being told at an early age that she was adopted. This revelation would lead her on a quest to find her biological parents and in the process, meet siblings she never knew existed. June's story is one that will warm your heart as she takes you on an amazing rollercoaster ride of suspense, intrigue, and revelations mingled with valuable lessons of faith, hope, and forgiveness. If you thought that happy endings are only found in fairy tales, "The Question Inside of Me An Adopted Daughter's Quest for Connection" will make you a believer that God hears our prayers and He is still in the miracle-working business.

First Lady Crisette Ellis
Greater Grace Temple, Detroit, MI

I have personally enjoyed my relationship with June Purifoy down through the years, seeing where she used to be, and where she is now. Her book, The Question Inside of Me - An Adopted Daughter's Quest for Connection, provides a roadmap to overcome challenges and circumstances in life. By offering an insider's perspective, June contrasts the longing of childless families desiring children, against the constant questions that often plague the adopted child. Her personal quest for connection placed her on a collision course with her biological parents' decision to give her up. June encourages us to remember that even when we have relentless questions, God is there to guide our human efforts.

Matthew Parker, President
The Summit Group

June Hawkins Purifoy has written a deeply personal, moving account of her quest to find her birth parents, and, in a sense, herself. During the long, hard journey she relies on her strength of character and unwavering faith to sustain her in moments of darkness and discouragement. I recommend her book not only to adoptees and their families but to anyone seeking to understand themselves in relationship to their parents and siblings better.

Brother Jerry Smith, OFM cap

This book is Dedicated to:

My Biological Mother & Father

In memory of my Parents
Charles Oliver Hawkins
&
Harriet Ruth Hawkins

In memory of
My Father-in-Love George L. Purifoy, Sr.
and Mother-in-Love Paralee Purifoy

Table of Contents

Endorsements 3
Acknowledgements 9
Prologue 13
Chapter One: Take A Look Inside 15
Chapter Two: Disconnected 23
Chapter Three: Chosen 35
Chapter Four: What About Me?! 41
Chapter Five: The Question Is? 51
Chapter Six: Help! I'm Trying to Find Myself 65
Chapter Seven: Damaged Goods 81
Chapter Eight: Rejection Can Be Direction 93
Chapter Nine: Connected by Grace 109
Chapter Ten: I'm God's Responsibility 123
Chapter Eleven: Complete in Him 135
Epilogue: My Steps Are Ordered 149
Bibliography 155
About the Author 159

Acknowledgements

I express my heartfelt thanks to all who provided comfort and support to me in writing my first book.

Thank you to my beautiful children, son, Frederick Jamal and daughter Camille Rachelle Aundra Purifoy. Without these blessings, I would not have known the importance and love of being a mother. A mother's love for her children is something that words cannot explain. It is endless; it's a unique ability that has been gifted by God. It is after having my children that I really had a hunger to search for my biological family.

I love my children, and especially my grandson Jamal Raymone Mitchell, who kept encouraging me to keep writing and constantly asking me is your book ready? I wish to thank my daughter-in-love, Geralyn, for her encouragement, ideas, and creativity and my granddaughters, Mawasi and Aliya. Thanks guys for going along with me to Build-A-Bear workshop. It was a lot of fun.

Thanks to my friends and confidantes (The Golden Girls) for your encouragement and diligent labor of love: Brenda Barnes, Gloria Bell, Natalie Cummings, Deborah Starr-Hodges, Sheila Phillips and Doris Thompson.

I wish to thank my prayer partner, Glady Sharper, who is a biological mother of five, a foster mother to many children, and an adoptive mother of four. I am thankful for your wisdom, guidance, and understanding that prayed me through.

I appreciate the support of some wonderful women of God, Stella Calloway and my neighbor, Ruby Greer for your proofreading techniques.

A thank you to two very special families, for sharing their joyous stories with me about their experiences in their process of adoption.

Thanks to my mentors, Mr. Matthew Parker, who helped to encourage me to get where I am today, and Bro. Jerry Smith, OFM cap, who took time with me and listened to my story and encouraged me in our Wednesdays, morning prayer with the word of God.

I want to give my First Lady, Crisette Ellis, a great big special thank you, for starting to stir in me the ability to write this book. Boot Camp V is where I received the confirmation to "stir up the gifts." I appreciate you for seeing something in me that I didn't see in myself.

I am grateful for Venus Theus and the Scribes for Christ who gave me the tools and instructions on writing. To always keep writing.

To Christina Dixon, I offer special thanks for her coaching ability, patience, and understanding to make my dream of publishing this book become a reality.

And last, but not least, to the memory of Beverly Cushman Johnson, who passed away in August 2009. Beverly was the young lady that worked at the high school where my biological mother and father had attended. She was the one that gave me the important information I needed to complete my search. Rest in Peace Beverly.

To God Be the Glory, for the things he hath done.

Prologue

We all have had questions, and some people still do? We want to know, *who am I? Where did I come from? Are these people who they say they are? Are they really my parents? Was I born into this family?* We have all asked these questions within ourselves. I believe this is a question that will go on into eternity.

For us, as adoptees, the question, *"Who am I?"* is always in our mind. Some adoptees have never had this question answered, and some may never want to know. As for me, I have always been an inquisitive person. I will ask someone a question in a minute. When, where, what, and most importantly why? I want to know.

Whenever I went to the doctor's office, they would ask me about my parents' medical backgrounds. I would say, "I am adopted. I don't know."

Some people, who are not adopted, are also asking this question. They do not know their biological mother or father. People today want to know where they come from, what nationally they are made from and many other questions. This is why ancestry.com is so popular because people want to know their families and their history.

For children given up for adoption, the absence of connection is real. It is a feeling that they are not always able to explain, but its presence remains inescapable. Birth mothers seek to avoid the pain and responsibility of parenting, while at the same time desiring to provide loving parents for a child they feel ill-equipped to raise. No matter how much love adoptive parents long to give an unwanted child, nothing erases the fact that the child wants to know the biological family. It is not a slight against the sacrifices of adoptive parents. It is just that all human beings desire to know from where they come.

After searching for many years, my search is over. My question has been answered. I found my biological parents. Hoping to connect with both families, it didn't happen as I thought. I waited 24 years.

As I share my quest to find my biological parents, I pray that others will realize that there is no way around the challenges of being an adoptee. Adoption is hard – for every person involved.

Many times, there are hurtful feelings on everyone's part. You can expect it. Those considering it would do wise to equip themselves to deal with it. That's why I'm sharing my story.

May God help you to prepare your heart to better support those around you who are young pregnant and afraid, who have been given up, or who long to make a difference in the life of a child.

There are some things inside of us that no one can touch, but God.

Chapter One

Take A Look Inside

> *"For I am fearfully and wonderfully made,*
> *Marvelous are thy works;"*
> Psalm 139:14 KJV

The miracle of a life coming into this world is amazing. When we are conceived in our mother's womb, it is our preparation for life. In the first trimester of pregnancy, the first seven weeks, the new individual receives chromosomes from each parent, therefore, becoming a unique human being, never to be repeated. A new person at this stage is a tiny living organism weighing only 15 ten-millionth of a gram. Life begins!

The First Trimester (Weeks 1-13)

During week three of the pregnancy, the individual starts to grow inside. Week four, the fertilized egg makes its way to the uterus. The cluster of cells divides into two parts, one that will form an embryo and the other a placenta. Week five, from conception the heart begins to beat, and the circulatory system starts to form. During this time, some women may be greeted with nausea and increased fatigue that women cope with during the first trimester. Week six, the face begins to form. The eyes, nose, mouth, and even a tongue start to form, and the little indentions on either side will become ears. Muscles are developing along the future spine. Arms and legs are budding. Week seven, brain cells are quickly developing. The brain has human proportions, and blood flows in veins. Week eight to eight ½, brain waves can be detected, and the unborn individual begins to swallow amniotic fluid. Fingers and toes are developing. Every organ is present, and the heartbeat is steady. The stomach produces digestive juices, the liver makes blood cells, and the kidneys begin to function. Fingerprints are engraved. Eyelids and the palms of hands become sensitive to touch. Week nine is special. The tiny life is no longer an embryo, but a fetus. At week 10 of pregnancy; the mother may still feel a little queasy. The unborn baby's body is sensitive to touch, and its eyelids, fingerprints and even fingernails are evident. Week 11, the individual practices breathing since they will have to breathe air immediately after birth. Vocal chords and taste buds form. Facial expressions and even smiles are evident.

Weeks 12-17, the gender of the individual can be visually determined. The distinctive characteristics begin to form, as fine hair grows on the upper lip, chin and eyebrows.

The Second Trimester (Weeks 14-27)

By week 14, the heart pumps several quarts of blood through the body every day. The eyebrows have formed, and eye movement can be detected. Week 15, the production of nerve cells begins and continues for a month. A second stage will occur at 25 weeks.

At four months, the individual is now only five ½ inches long, weighing approximately five ounces, is actively moving about inside the safety of the womb and can turn, kick and even do somersaults, which can now be felt by the mother. Bone marrow is now beginning to form, and the heart is pumping 25 quarts of blood a day.

At four ½ months, the nostrils and toenails become visible. At the end of the fourth month, the baby's ears are functioning and can hear the mother's heartbeat, as well as external noises like music. The baby is also able to experience pain. Life-saving surgery has been successfully performed on babies at this age.

At five-six months, each side of the brain now has a billion nerve cells. Thumb-sucking has been observed during the fifth month. The baby practices breathing by inhaling amniotic fluid into its developing lungs. The baby will increase seven times in weight and nearly double in length. The baby's weight is about 640g (22oz.), and 23cm (9") long. Fine hair grows on eyebrows and head, and eyelash fringe appears. Babies born at this age have survived.

The Third Trimester (Weeks 28-42)

By 27-32 weeks from conception, the baby can recognize the mother's voice. The baby is using four of the five senses (vision, hearing, taste, and touch), opens and closes the eyes and can relate to the moods of the mother.

At eight months, the baby's skin becomes pink and smooth. The pupils of the eyes respond to light. The weight has increased by 1 kg (over two pounds) and the living quarters inside the mother's womb are becoming cramped. The baby's fingernails reach to the tip of the finger. The skin begins to thicken, with a layer of fat stored underneath for insulation and nourishment. The baby swallows a gallon of amniotic fluid each day and often hiccups. The mother may be able to feel an elbow or heel against her abdomen as the baby's movement becomes limited, due to the cramped quarters causing the baby's kicks to become stronger.

Nine months (33-42 weeks)

By 33-42 weeks from conception, the baby gains about one-half pound per week as he/she prepares for birth. The bones in the child's head are soft and flexible to more easily mold for the journey down the birth canal. The baby triggers labor and birth occurs, an average of 264-270 days after conception. Of the 45 generations of cell divisions before adulthood, 41 have already taken place. Only four more come before adolescence. Ninety percent of a person's development happens in the womb. What a miracle!

Science tells us that human life begins at the time of conception. From the moment fertilization takes place, the child's genetic makeup is already complete. Its gender has already been determined, along with its length and hair, eye and skin color. You have a human egg and a human sperm, and their sole purpose in life is to meet each other and fuse, to create a one cell human being. The only thing the embryo needs to become a fully functioning being is the time to grow and develop. *"For you created my inmost being: you knit me together in my mother's womb." Psalm 139:13 NIV*

The baby makes its grand entrance into this world, without knowing anything or anybody. We come into this world depending on someone to take care of us for everything. The baby has been in a safe womb for nine months and depended on the mother for all their needs. Those nine months develop a special bonding with the mother and baby.

Before being cut, the umbilical cord, which runs from an opening in the baby's stomach to the placenta in the womb, carries oxygen and nutrients from the mother to the baby, is clamped about 3-4cm from the baby's belly button with a plastic clip. Then, soon after the baby is born, it's cut between the two clamps, leaving a stump on the baby's tummy, thus forming the baby's belly button.

When the baby is born, it is an exciting time as a new member is added to the family. Everyone has been waiting and wanting to see this new life; wanting to know if it's a boy or girl, who they look like, the child's name and many other things. It's exhilarating!!!

Things are a little different when a baby is to be adopted. I feel sorry for the biological mother. After going through nine months of carrying this unborn baby in her body, then after the baby's birth, it is given up for adoption. The choice has been made. We can choose many things in life, our careers, our spouses, the activities we want to get involved in, and our friends. But one thing we cannot choose is our biological mother and father.

Choosing Between Abortion or Adoption

Choosing between abortion or adoption can be the decision of a lifetime. Both abortion or adoption are emotionally difficult choices for a woman to make. When a woman finds out she is pregnant; there are 3 options available. 1) She can give birth to the baby and raise it until they become an adult. 2) She can give birth to the baby and place the baby to be adopted and 3) She can end the pregnancy by having an abortion.

Some women facing an unplanned pregnancy believe that if they have an abortion, that is the easier way out, its fast and painless, and no one will have ever known of the pregnancy. Women may have difficulty emotionally accepting their abortion decision and may later experience postpartum depression or post-abortion stress syndrome (PASS). PASS can last for several years, sometimes longer and may manifest itself in symptoms such as anxiety, depression, flashbacks and even suicidal thoughts in extreme cases.

When choosing adoption, this gives the baby a gift of life. Hopefully, good adoptive parents who may otherwise have no chance of becoming parents can provide a good childhood, and the birth mother gets a better chance of moving on from this difficult time in her life. Adoption offers a means of providing a pregnant woman with an alternative home for her child, offers a solution for a couple who cannot have children of their own, and provides a child with a family that is better equipped to raise the child than the one in which the child was born. There are now family agencies or organizations that will help through the process. An adoption can also be kept confidential, where her family or friends won't know about it.

Planned Parenthood's report states that from October 1, 2011, to September 30, 2012, the organization performed 327,166 abortions and only 2,197 adoption referrals. That equals just one adoption for every 149 abortions.

I feel sorry for the unborn babies that didn't make it, because of abortion. Abortion is legal in America now through all nine months. A sad irony is over two million couples wait to adopt, and that includes children of all races and those with special needs.

Adoptees, may not like who our adoptive parents are, but we should be glad our biological mothers gave us life. In fact, everyone that is reading this should be glad that you were given life.

If you choose to place the baby up for adoption, your pregnancy ends in giving life!

If you choose to give your baby up for an abortion, your pregnancy ends with death!

"The two most important days in your life are, the day you are born. and the day when you find out why." - Mark Twain

Chapter Two

Disconnected

"But when it pleased God, who separated me from my mother's womb, and called me by his grace."
Galatians 1:15 KJV

Disconnecting from the umbilical cord, starts the baby to become their own individual. We are all very thankful when our babies are born healthy and with all their limbs and organs in place.

There are a couple of bonding experiences that the birth mother has with the baby right after the birth. One is after the baby is born and cleaned up, the baby is placed on the mother's stomach, close to her chest and heart. Another great connection is the newborn's natural instinct to be drawn to the mother's breast for the milk. After each one of my children was born, the first day or hours, they wanted to suck on my breast for their feeding. That was a special time for the mother and her baby.

When the baby is going to be adopted, the birth mother and the newborn are not allowed to experience breastfeeding. In fact, the birth mother does not even get a chance to see her baby; it is taken away from her immediately after it is born. The mother and child may never see one another again.

Some children are adopted later on in their life, due to abuse or neglect or other circumstances. Each situation has its characteristics as well as its risks

It is so good to know, that when we come into this world that we are no accident. God has a purpose and plan for each one of us.

> *"You know me inside and out, you know every bone in my body; you know exactly how I was made bit by bit, how I was sculpted from nothing into something." Psalm 139:15-The Message*

The biological mother still names the baby when it is born; And when the adoptive parents adopt the baby or child, they may choose to change the name.

Closed and Open Adoptions

Today, there are closed and open adoptions. In open adoptions, the birth parents and adoptive parents have met, exchange information and some continue their contact and communicate after the adoption process has taken place. Open adoption began in the 1980's because it is believed to help both the adoptees and the adoptive parents with a healthy psychological development. In closed adoptions, the identity of the birth parents is not revealed to the adoptive parents or to the child. When I was adopted, it was a closed adoption

The disconnection and separation start the process of the child now being a ward of the court, in the State's custody. The parents have relinquished their parental rights, and the state has given the child to a children's agency.

Some birth parents may give consent directly to the adoptive parents. Independent adoptions are legal in almost all states and some like it better, because long waiting time may be avoided and agency standards do not apply.

Michigan was one of the few states prior to 1995, that required a court termination of the rights of the birth parents before the child could be placed for adoption. The law required that the placement of a child with an unrelated individual or couple could only be done by a state-licensed child-placing agency or by the Michigan Department of Human Services. Placement of an infant directly from the hospital with prospective adoptive parents required licensing the adoptive parents as foster parents. A court-appointed guardian must act on behalf of any emancipated minor parent who consents to an adoption of a child or who releases a child to a child-placing agency for adoption. By my birth parents being teenagers and considered minors, their parents had to act on their behalf.

After 1995, Michigan's adoption laws have been modified. It is possible to make a "temporary placement" of a child in a prospective adoptive home, immediately following birth, while the legal proceedings are completed.

The prospective adoptive parents petition the court to adopt a specific child. The petition is filed in the county court where the child is found or where the adoptive parents reside. The court orders an investigation to assure that the interests of the adopted child are protected.

Following a completed report of investigation and satisfied that the adopted child's best interests are served, the court will issue an order terminating the rights of the parent, the child-placing agency, court or the Department of Human Services (DHS). The court makes the adopted child a ward of the court, orders placement in an adoption and assigns a child-placing agency, DHS or an agent of the court to supervise/monitor the adoptive placement. After the child has been in placement for about one year, the court may find it in the adopted child's best interest for the court to enter an order of adoption. The order of adoption completes the process. The adoption makes the adopted child an heir of the adoptive parents, and in the eyes of the law, this child is as much a child of the adopting parents as one who would have been born to the parents.

The family name of the adoptive parent may or may not become the name of the adopted child at the discretion of the parties. The courts notify the department of community health of the adoption permitting the department to issue a new birth certificate in the adoptive parents' name. My adoptive parents changed my name from the one my biological mother chose for me. In the 1950's when I was adopted, I didn't get a birth certificate and still I do not have one, all I have is a registrar of birth from Lansing, Michigan

At the time of adoption, written non-identifying information about the adopted child's health history and family background is made available to the adoptive parents. Identifying information is withheld unless the birth parents and the prospective adoptive parents agree to exchange identifying information.

I was placed in the foster care of the Children's Aid Society in Detroit, Michigan. My adoptive mother told me how they applied and passed all inspections of the home for them to adopt a child and the process began. I was not legally adopted until one year later, which was 1956.

Families with Adopted Children

I know of several families that have adopted children, and all the adoptions have been successful. In one family, the adoptive parents already had five biological children. Later, they became Foster Parents. They love caring for children. The adoptive mother told me how she had many children that came in and out of their home. They took in all types of children with problems and special needs. Five of these children were very special to them, and they adopted the five. Two came to them when they were babies. The other three were siblings, two girls, and one boy.

The boy and one of the girls are twins. They came to them when they were around five or six years old. The children had been in several different foster homes but wanted to be a part of this family. The adoptive parents had the children for around two years, after that the state had placed them for adoption. They knew their biological mother and had lived with her until Child Protective Services took them away because of abuse and neglect. This mother's parental rights were terminated. When the children were placed for adoption, this family enjoyed having the children with them and loved them very much, so they agreed to adopt them. The three are grown now and have families of their own and are doing well. Their biological mother got herself together, and they always have kept in touch with her, and she is still a part of their lives.

The next two families that I know have adopted children, within the last 18 years. I am very close to both families. We'll call one the Jones family and the other family will be called the Smiths.

The Jones family already has three girls, but always wanted a boy. This family told me about 2 years prior to starting the adoption process that a visiting prophet came to their church and stated to her husband that he was going to have a son and this son was going to be a covenant between God and her husband.

Many months later, her Bishop prophesied to her that he saw her having a son but did not see her giving birth to him. He stated that she was going to adopt him.

The Jones family made a decision to start the adoption process. They contacted several adoption agencies to see if they had any children available. They were looking for a newborn baby boy. The majority of adoptive parents want to adopt newborn babies, so they can lay the foundation for the child. One of the adoption agencies did not have (at that time) newborn infants; they were more of an agency that placed special needs children or children from abusive homes into temporary foster homes. Some of these children eventually become available for adoption but are usually around three years old or older. The Joneses selected one agency that they felt would work well with them. They completed the paperwork and started a series of interviews. A social worker was assigned to them to interview, performed a background check and came to the home to do a home assessment.

When the worker comes to the home, they want to make sure that the home has enough space to add another child. There are space requirements that the state requires each child to have in the home. After all of the requirements were met they were made foster parents. The Joneses stated they had to be licensed as foster parents first before the agency placed any child in the home.

The adoption agency contacted the Joneses and said they had a young lady that was pregnant and wanted to place her baby for adoption. The Joneses became excited. The next step was to complete a family album that told stories about the family, each person in the home and had to have family pictures. They had to explain what they liked to do, as well as their values and beliefs. They said this was to give the birth mother a good idea about the family she was giving her baby up to. The birth mothers look at several family albums before making a selection. The Joneses submitted their family album.

Later they learned that the birth mother decided not to put her baby up for adoption and then learned that she had a baby girl. Some birth mothers change their minds about giving their baby up for adoption; especially after she begins to feel the baby's movement. Two months later they received a call that two baby boys (twins) were in foster care. They were six weeks old, and they were available for adoption. The Joneses were nervous and contemplated saying no to two new babies. They prayed about it, and consulted with their Pastors and decided to proceed to the next step.

The next step was to go visit the babies at their foster home. They had a pleasant visit with the foster mom and the babies. They were beautiful boys, and they knew they had to proceed with getting them into their home.

They completed all of the paperwork and really wanted the babies to come home before Christmas, but because the birth parents delayed signing away their parental rights, the twins could not come home until late January.

The agency could not tell the Joneses in advance when the babies were coming home but warned them that it would be sudden and quick. Sure enough, they received a phone call the day before they were supposed to come home. Mrs. Jones left work that evening and had to go shopping to get all of the baby supplies they needed. They met with the social worker and the birth mother. It was their first time meeting the birth mother, who was a pleasant woman that loved the babies deeply. She held the babies over each shoulder as she gave the Joneses instructions on how to raise her sons. Mrs. Jones stated that watching tears flow down the birth mother's face as she tells them to tell the babies that she loved them and to raise them to love God and not to give them spankings. Mrs. Jones said that broke her heart so much that she became so confused. For a moment, she wondered if she should go through with the adoption or let the birth mother keep the babies, and begin the process over with another child. Mrs. Jones was so conflicted that she started crying too. Mrs. Jones made a promise to the birth mother and told her that she would raise them the way she stated, and to this day she has honored her promise to the birth mother and has done a wonderful job in raising all of her children, not just with the boys but also with her daughters.

The birth mother proceeded to hand Mrs. Jones the babies one by one, and there wasn't a dry eye in the room. It was such an emotional moment. The social worker asked if she could take some pictures with the babies in case they want to see what she looks like when they are older. The birth mother refused and left the room. The Joneses waited for her to return but eventually saw her driving away. The birth mother left the agency without saying goodbye.

Mrs. Jones told me how she has respect for the birth mothers who make one of the toughest decision anyone can make. They have enough courage to know that they could not take care of their children. They have enough love to want to give their children the best. They have enough strength to go through the adoption process, find a home for their babies and love them enough to let them go. Mrs. Jones stated that her heart was so full that she promised to be the best mom she could to them because she knows that is what the birth mother wanted.

The birth mother of the boys had carried the babies for 36 weeks without anyone knowing she was pregnant. She did not know she was pregnant with twins until she gave birth. When the birth mother's family learned later that she had placed the babies for adoption, they were furious. They wanted the boys, but it was too late. The social worker called Mrs. Jones and told her that the birth mother came to the adoption agency every day for weeks crying and asking for her babies back. It was too late! The social worker asked Mrs. Jones to write a letter to the birth mother and send the letter with some pictures of the boys. Mrs. Jones said she wrote a 10-page handwritten letter thanking her for her courage, love, and strength to place her children in her care. Mrs. Jones also sent the birth mother pictures of the boys at various stages of growth and development, and each picture showed how much they were loved and how happy they were (smiles in every picture). After the birth mother received the letter and pictures, she stopped asking for them and stopped contacting the adoption agency. The social worker stated that sometimes this happens and when the birth mother receives the letter and pictures she can see that the children are doing well and she made the right decision. This proved to be true because they never heard from the birth mother again.

The Smith family is a couple who didn't have any children. With patience and much prayer, they decided to adopt. They went to a Christian adoption agency and started the process. It was the beginning of a wonderful journey for them. The Smith's said they were also assigned to a counselor who held sessions with other couples who had decided to adopt. The sessions allowed them to bond with other couples who were looking to adopt, which made the experience that much more enjoyable. To this day, the Smith's said that they keep in contact with the other couples and they all are now proud parents.

The Smith's adopted a baby girl. Their adoption gave them a feeling of indescribable joy that cannot be put into words.

The adoption process for them went very well. The Smith's met with the biological mother on six or seven different occasions. The biological mother told them about the biological father, but they never had an opportunity to meet him. The biological mother was a single mom who already had two daughters and one son. The thought of raising another child was too overwhelming for her, so she turned to the adoption agency for help. That was the Smith's beginning of a miraculous journey.

There are all types of situations and circumstances where people are still adopting children. I pray that they are welcomed into homes that show them love like I was.

I was reading online on TODAY.com about a year ago, of how a 92-year-old woman adopts a 76-year-old daughter. After decades of considering themselves mother and daughter, two women finally made it official. The 92-year-old woman longs to call the 76-year-old her daughter.

The ladies are actually cousins, but the older woman began raising the younger lady, when she was about 13 or 14, after her father died of a heart attack, and her mother suffered from mental illness, leaving her unable to take care of her daughter.

The older lady took her in and started raising her as her child. "She always fit in beautifully." The senior woman said she had always wanted to adopt the young cousin but didn't want to upset the biological mother, who died several years ago.

"The senior woman stated as "she has gotten older, it's kind of like my life is a beautiful jigsaw puzzle, but there was a piece missing."

That is the same way I had felt for a long time. There was a piece of my life missing.

Chapter Three

Chosen

"His unchanging plan has always been to adopt us into His own family by sending Jesus Christ to die for us."

Ephesians 1:5 – Good News

More than 3,000 children in Michigan are waiting for permanent loving homes to call their own. I'm glad that I was one, that was chosen.

Adoption is not a substitute for having a biological child nor is it a way of "replacing" a child who dies. Adoption is one of the many ways to make a family.

My adoptive mother started telling me the story of how I was adopted when I was around three or four years old, at least that is the time I can remember. After I was born, I was placed in the care of the Children's Aid Society. I was told I was in there for approximately 10 to 15 days before I was placed in their home for adoption. My adoptive parents told me how they had looked at several baby girls, but they felt the babies were not the right match they wanted. They had agreed on adopting a baby girl.

My adoptive mother told me that one day they received a call from a social worker at the Children's Aid Society, stating they had a baby girl up for adoption, and asking if they would like to come in to see her. My adoptive mother told me that the call she received that day, she felt was a very special call. They made an appointment at the Children's Aid Society a couple of days later to see me.

They went for their scheduled appointment. The social worker allowed them to read my profile first and told them a little about the biological families' backgrounds. The worker brought me into the room, and my adoptive mother stated that at first sight, she knew I was the baby for them. She told me how she and my adoptive father held me and looked at me really good. She looked behind my ears to see if I was going to be any darker than what I was. After spending some time with me, they said I was the one. The next couple of days after their visit, they brought their parents, their sisters, and brothers to look at me too. They all agreed, I was the one.

My adoptive parents petitioned the court to adopt me. The court has the authority to resolve any custody disputes that arise between temporary placement and formal placement. The court receives the consent to adopt and other required legal forms. The court will order an investigation and will review the investigation report to assure that the adoption is in the best interest of the adopted child. The court will terminate the rights of the parents. (Note the rights of both parents must be terminated by the court before formal placement). The process of the order of adoption started.

My adoptive mother told me when Children's Aid Society called them and told them they could pick me up in two days; they had to hurry and go shopping for baby items. Hudson's Department store in the Northland Mall in Southfield, MI., had just opened and they went out and bought all kinds of baby items. They said they had been waiting for this time. My adoptive mother always told me, I was the special child they had been praying, waiting and asking God for.

I was placed in a loving home with wonderful adoptive parents. There was a supervision period for about one year. The court appointed a social worker to oversee the adjustment of the family and me, during the period of supervision. Upon completion of the supervisory period, the court entered a final order of adoption completing the legal process.

The Teddy Bears

My adoptive mother would read to me different fairy tale stories each night. I always enjoyed the story of *Goldilocks & The Three Bears*. It was one of my favorite stories. She would use the three Teddy Bears to tell me how I was adopted.

Teddy Bears are among the favorite gifts for children. Often given to adults to signify love, congratulations or sympathy, we purchase teddy bears as crib toys for babies. Young men buy them and give them to their girlfriends as a token of affection. They are used for tokens of solace in police cars, hospitals and now when a person has been killed; they place a teddy bear on the certain site where the victims have died.

When we look at children's stories, teddy bears are a popular icon. Teddy bears make us feel comfortable. We all have had the experience of cuddling up with a stuffed bear. Teachers are still finding this beloved stuffed animal to be a great learning tool in classrooms.

Teddy Bears are still popular today. A "Build-A-Bear" Workshop, Inc. was developed in 1997, by founder Maxine Clark and is a teddy bear themed experience retail store. The America Retailer headquartered in Overland, Missouri sells teddy bears and other stuffed animals. By 2007, the store had sold over 50 million bears and had over 400 stores in the United States and other countries. The teddy bear themed experience retail store is where a child or adult is inspired to create their own huggable companion. You can choose your very own stuffed animal and imagine how you want to personalize it as your very own. There are hundreds of outfits and accessories to choose to dress up and create. Each Build-A-Bear experience is new, and every bear begins a story.

My story of the Three Bears was told to me when I was around the age of three or four years old, by my adoptive mother telling me how I was adopted. She would use the illustration of the teddy bears. The story would start with my adoptive parents being two very lonely people without a baby or child in the home. They were trying to think what to do to make their home a special place for a family. The two bears went to the hospital, (she had three teddies bears that symbolized the mother, the father, and myself) and picked out this baby bear. She would tell me how the mother and father bear adopted this very special cute girl bear and brought the baby bear home. The mother and father bears were so excited and happy that now they have a baby bear that belongs to them and they can keep it.

I didn't understand the meaning of the story at the time, but she told it to me several times and always used the illustration of the bears, which made it, over time, more and more believable. The teddy bear story was my start in knowing I was adopted.

I remember as a little girl having a teddy bear. I believe after she told me about being adopted, the teddy bear started being a comfort to me. I remember carrying my teddy bear everywhere with me until I started school. My teddy bear got so raggedy that the stuffing started coming out of the arm. The teddy bear was like having something that belonged to me that I could hold on to. I loved when she read stories to me about the teddy bears which had the meaning of the family.

Teddy bears are created and chosen as an imaginary friend or companion. After I started growing up, my adoptive mother still used the story of the teddy bears to tell me how I was adopted. I still love teddy bears to this day.

It feels special to be chosen. When I was a teenager, we had a saying that when a young man chooses a young lady for his girlfriend, they would say, you have been chosen. That would make you feel very special to know someone picked you out amongst many, to be their special friend and there would be no one else as special as you.

Chosen by God

Every individual in this world has a purpose and destiny that God has chosen for you to do. *"For he chose us in Him before the creation of the world." Ephesians 1:4, NIV.* God chose us before the foundations of the earth. Before the worlds were ever formed, He knew you and me and has a great plan and purpose for us. He didn't create us to be average or just to get by in life. He created us to excel! Not only did He choose us, but He has equipped us with everything we need to live an abundant life.

When my adoptive parents picked me out, it was all ordained by God. He chose me to be the baby girl that they planned for and wanted. Of course, I didn't realize God's plan nor did I see this for my life, until finding my biological family. One of my prayers is "God, help me to see myself the way You see me." When I came to God and gave my life to Him, I already belonged to Him. I was not chosen because I came; I came because I was chosen. I am chosen by God, and I am blessed.

Chapter Four

What About Me?!
*"For thou art my hope, O Lord God:
Thou art my trust from my youth."*
                                              Psalm 71:5 KJV

Growing up, I had a wonderful childhood. Most of which was spent at church and school. I can remember when I was three years old going to a church on Conant Street in Detroit, Michigan. I was brought up in the Church of God Reformation under the pastorate of the late Rev. Dr. Raymond S. Jackson. After we were there, I remember my parents talking about the members of the Conant Church of God were working on building a new church on Joseph Campau. We went to the site almost every day when they started building this church. My adoptive father and most of the men of the church helped build it. The ladies of the church cooked and brought food and water to the men daily. I remember watching them put in the pews, lay down the tile in the sanctuary, and put in the basement steps. It was a lot of fun for me as a little girl being around this church building and watching it built from the ground up. In 1959, the church was completed, and we had our first service in October 1959. The church, Joseph Campau

Avenue Church of God, 17401 Joseph Campau, Detroit, Michigan 48212 is alive and going strong today, under the leadership of Rev. David Lunn.

We were always at church on Sunday's for Sunday school, morning and evening worship. Most Sunday's we had an afternoon program at 3:30 p.m. When I was around 11 or 12 years old, I started going to the youth hour, which began at 6:00 p.m. Then we would go right into the evening worship at 7:30 p.m. We were in church on Sundays all day long.

On Wednesday night's we went to mid-week prayer service and whatever meetings that were scheduled during the week. I don't remember having a babysitter to come to our home and sit with me for anything. If my parents were involved, I had to go too.

The church members felt like family to me. The older adult members were Uncles and Aunts and the children I felt like cousins to me. Most families in the church had two or more children and I, along with one of my best girlfriends, were the only child in our families. The two us became close friends, and to this day we still call each other "sister."

I had fun being with all the children around the church. I always had somebody to play with. In the 1950's-1960's, parents brought their children to church and made them stay through all the services. But, when all the services were dismissed, and everyone was going home, I had to go home alone. It started me to thinking, *"why don't I have any brothers or sisters to go home with us. Why do I have to go home to an empty house? Is it because I am adopted, and I'm not supposed to be with this family? Do I have brothers and sisters somewhere else?"*

To get my mind off of being alone, my mother kept me active in church and other events. I participated in all the Christmas and Easter programs. When I was around eight years old, we had a singing group that I was in with three other young girls from the church, and we had the same name as the older group, except we were the Junior Silverton's. The musician of the church started our group, after admiring our mentors who were an older teenage group of young ladies from our church. Our group would sing at our church for different services, and we also had singing engagements at other churches. I was glad to be in the group because it made me feel like I belonged to something or someone. I also became involved with the Junior Ushers and participated in the Youth Choir.

We had a great youth choir at the church. But the only thing was we didn't have a certain Sunday when the choir could sing because the majority of us had not made a commitment to Jesus Christ. They would let us sing for Easter and Christmas Programs, or once maybe twice we would do a concert. The ministers would ask us, how could we sing to the congregation about coming to Christ, when we have not accepted him as our Lord and Savior. So, one day the young people got together and agreed that the next Sunday, all of us were going to the altar and we were going to get saved. I think I was around 14 years old. Well, Sunday came, and I went to the altar, but I wasn't playing, something got a hold of me, and I knew the Lord had saved me. It was an awesome feeling. We all were crying and repenting. That was my first encounter with the Lord. Many times, after that, I would re-dedicate my life.

I started to like going to church then, because again, I had a feeling of belonging, and being around people who felt like family. Most Sunday's I would go home with some of my friends from the church or my mother would let them come home with me. She was very good about letting me have company or letting me go with some of the families from the church. I know it was because she didn't want me to be alone so much.

I remember when I was around the church playing with different ones, that one of the young people came up to me and said, "June, I didn't know you were adopted by the Hawkins's, and they are not your real parents!"

I would answer yeah; I knew I was adopted. I was so glad that my parents told me, even when I was too young to understand. I would remember the Teddy Bears. Although it really didn't hurt me when they would make those statements, it made me feel like an outcast. The question inside of me would rise up and started me to thinking again. *"Who do I belong to? Who is my real mother? Who is my real father?"* After those thoughts, would run across my mind, I would let it pass and move on.

My adoptive father was a very smart and skillful man. He never went to college, but he did finish high school. So, did my adoptive mother, she finished high school and was a great homemaker, who would sew, cook, and kept a manicured yard. My adoptive mother never did any work outside of the home. When they were building the church, my father, did the architectural work and the blueprint drawing. He not only did that type of work for the Joseph Campau church but for many other churches that were being built or remodeled. He began the Joseph Campau Ave. Church of God Credit Union, the Joseph Campau Printing Press and many other things he did at the church.

Starting School

At the age of five, I started kindergarten at the now-closed Courville Elementary School on Nevada in Detroit, Michigan. I went there from Kindergarten to the sixth grade. To me, when I first walked into that school it was huge. The Kindergarten only went to school for half of the day. When I started, I went in the afternoon. My mother would walk me to school every day and come back and pick me up. I enjoyed those days at my elementary school because there again; it gave me a chance to be around other children and make some friends.

When I started the first grade, I was glad to be in school a full day. My mother would walk me to school in the mornings, and she would come back at noon, walk me home for lunch, then walk me back to school and walk me back home in the afternoons. My mother kept her driver's license, but she never would keep the car nor would she drive. We would always walk or take the bus when she and I would go places. Sometimes a relative or someone from the church would come by and take me to school or pick me up. My mother never did any work outside of the home, and my father worked two jobs during most of my childhood.

Starting the second grade, she would let me walk to school by myself along with other children in the neighborhood. Thank goodness it was only four short blocks from home. Because my mother was a homemaker, I could come home for lunch even in the winter months when we had snow storms. I came home for lunch and went right back to school. The bad part about those days when I was in elementary and middle school, is that when it was cold, and it snowed, girls could not wear pants to school and you could not wear boots in school. When girls did wear pants, they were just to be worn under your dress or skirt, and the boots were boots that fit over our shoes. If you had those things on when you got in the school before you went into your classroom you had to take them off. Very few times did my mother give me money to stay at school for lunch. She would have to send a note requesting that I stay for lunch at school for that day. She was always there for me. When I came home, she would have my lunch ready and on the table. And at the end of the school day, she would be there when I got home, asking me how my day was at school and had a snack waiting for me. If she had to go anywhere, she would try to do it during the times I was in school and make sure she was back home when I got out of school. She didn't give me a key until I was in middle school, but still, she was there at home waiting for me.

When I was in elementary school, I didn't feel so much of not belonging or thought about being adopted, because I became active in school also. I was a Girl Scout, was in the Glee Club, started taking piano lessons, and learned how to roller skate and went skating at least once a week. With all the activities, I was involved with at church and school; it would take my mind off of my adoption. There were some kids in elementary school that had it rough at home. They wore the same old clothes every day to school. Some girls didn't have their hair comb, their clothes were dirty, and they had holes in their shoes. Some boys had what they called the ringworms. So, seeing them in these circumstances took my mind off of myself, and I started feeling sorry for some of the other kids.

All throughout those past years, she would remind me of the Teddy Bears and me being adopted and how I was chosen to be their child. She started telling me about the adolescent years and how I was starting to develop into womanhood and about how babies are conceived and born. Every now and then, a thought would come to my mind about women having children, mothers, and fathers.

At this stage in my life, I started asking my mother and father, "Why am I the only child? Why didn't they adopt any more children? and did they try to have any children?" My mother explained to me that due to their past illness they could not have any children together. She said they thought about adopting another child shortly after they had adopted me but just didn't do it.

My parents, especially my father, were very strict. I could not look at American Bandstand. I go to the movie theater (we called it "the show" back then), no parties (except for those given by the young people at the church), baseball or basketball games and a lot of other things he didn't want me to do. I was surprised he let me go skating. But at the time, when I first learned how to skate, they only played organ music, and my father enjoyed skating too.

When I would come home from school, I would turn on the TV to American Bandstand and watch it until I heard him pulling up in the driveway, then I would turn to another channel. My mother was a little more lenient than my father. She would tell me when I would ask to go the show, that she was not giving me permission to go, but she did know where I was. Little by little my father would give in. When I would get my allowance every week, I would go to the record shop and buy myself a 45 record. I had a good record collection in the early 60's especially with Motown Sounds being in Detroit and going strong. Every year the Motown Revues would be at the Fox theater around Christmas time when we would have our Christmas break from school. My cousins would always go, and my mother started letting me go with them, but we wouldn't tell my father.

After I turned 11 years old, my father became a little more lenient. He started letting me go places, and he would take me, as long as I had a friend or relative to go with me.

Both my adoptive parent's families always treated me like a family member. Both sides never said or acted toward me like I was not a part of the family. They treated me well. I had twin cousins that I was always around. We spent a lot of time together as we were growing up. When they would grow out of their clothes, I would get some things and my best friend, who was also an only child, would get some of their clothes too. So, we really called ourselves sisters when we wore my twin cousin clothes.

When I went to Middle School, my uncle would come and pick me up every day and take me to school to make sure I got there safely. I appreciated both sides of the family because as of this day no one has ever mentioned anything to me about being adopted.

Chapter Five

The Question Is?
"Who Is My Mother?"
Matthew 12:48 KJV

The year of 1966, we moved on the northwest side of Detroit. My parents wanted a bigger home for me to entertain my friends and for me to go to a better school for my education.

I finished the 6th grade at Courville School, and our class was to have our graduation in January of 1966. Our class didn't have our graduation because of a snowstorm that week. We had almost 22" inches of snow that year. (I will never forget that week). Everything was canceled and closed down. In the 60's the semesters would go from September to January and January to June. You could start school or graduate in January.

Things were starting to change that year, not only for me, but things at our church were also changing. Some of my peer's families moved out of state, and some families became members of other churches. It is good to know that some of the people I grew up with are still members of the church today.

Changes were taking place in me. I started to develop more physically and mentally. I was no longer interested in playing with toys or dolls but became interested in meeting boys. I became concerned about how I looked and what types of clothes I wore. I started a new school that year, which we called Junior High School back then, now it's called Middle School. I was a little afraid of being in a new classroom with people I didn't know. The name of the school was Vernor on Pembroke on the Northwest side of Detroit. It was both an elementary and junior high school. The junior high school classes went from grades seven to nine.

We moved into a new home located in a predominately white neighborhood. There were very few blacks in the neighborhood and very few in the school. I had to make some adjustments. Thoughts started coming to my mind that had me wondering if my biological mother or father lived in this neighborhood, will some of the children in this neighborhood be my biological sisters or brothers, or maybe the school that I will be attending, will some of the children there be part of my biological family? All kinds of questions and thoughts kept coming to my mind, especially when this is all new surroundings for me.

When starting this new school, the classes were a little more advanced than what I had been taught. Again, my mother was always there for me. When I would come home and tell her how I was struggling in school, she would take time to help me with homework and studying.

My mother started talking with me more about relationships, marriages, children and basically about life. When I became 12 years old, she would tell me, if I wanted to know about my biological mother and father, she would make an appointment at the Children's Aid Society to see what information they would give me. I heard what she was saying, but the first couple of times she mentioned it, I didn't think too much of it, and I just let it pass. Several months later, I thought about what she said. I think she could tell what I was feeling by the questions I started asking her.

After being in a new school for a couple of months, I became interested in boys. I got a lot of attention from the boys at school and at church. One particular boy that got my attention was our paper boy. We had been in our new home for a couple of months when one day, the doorbell rang. When I went to open the door, it was the paperboy and his friend. He asked for my mother or father because he wanted to collect. When my mother went to the door, he asked my mother, if he could talk with me and she told him yes. She called me to the door. He said hello and told me his name, and I told him mine, then he asked if he could have my phone number because he wanted to call me to get to know me better, so I gave it to him. I was only 12 years old, but I could have passed for the age of 15 or 16. I was so excited about meeting this young boy. That same night he called me, and he told me about himself, and I told him about me. I saw him in school a couple of times but we didn't do much talking then, we did more talking on the phone. He asked if he could come over and I had to ask my mother if I could start having boy company. Before my mother would let him come over to visit me, she wanted some more background information about him. One good thing she knew was that he was the paperboy for our block, which meant he had a job. She knew his name, where he lived, and his phone number. She had to know a little about his parents, where they lived, what was their occupations were and what church they attended? After she did all of this investigating, she told me, yes; he could come over only on Friday's or Saturday's. I was happy because now she was letting me have boy company. He came over a couple of times, and we would listen to music on the record player and dance, but we talked on the phone mostly every night. After we became friends, he told me that he heard it was a new girl on the block and she was cute and wanted to meet me. He finally asked me to "go with him?" which meant, I would be his girlfriend. I was chosen. I told him yes! He and I became close, and we enjoyed each other's company. We would go to the mall, movies, bowling; he was the first one to teach me how to bowl and a lot of other places together. I wanted to teach him how to skate because I loved skating and he didn't know how to skate. We never did get around to that. Sometimes he would go to church with me.

As our friendship grew, I became close with his family, which consisted of his mother, his father, and one sister. I wondered to myself at times, *Could this be my biological brother? Or a cousin? Could I be related to his family biologically?* Different questions would repeatedly enter my mind about my biological family.

After being close in friendship with him and his family, I told him about my being adopted. I asked him was there any children that he knew of in his family given up for adoption? He asked his mother and father, and they said, "No." He was one of the first of my friends to ask me "How does it feel to know that your adoptive parents are not your real parents?" I told him, "I felt that they are the only parents that I know who are very wonderful to me and they are my real parents."

It had me thinking more about who was the real woman that gave birth to me and gave me up for adoption? Who is the man that impregnated her and they conceived me? Every now and then I wondered, *"Did I have any brothers or sisters? Was I the only child she had? Was she or he a family member on my adoptive mother side or father side that no one told me about?"* This was when I told my mother that I wanted to go to the Children's Aid Society and talk with someone about my adoption.

I did some research on adoption, and the research showed that adopted children, during adolescence or early adulthood, often initiate searches for the birth parents.

I was 13 years old, and my mother told me she would call and make an appointment for me to talk with a social worker. I wanted to get some information about my biological parents. The first time she made the appointment, I told her to cancel it. I became fearful and afraid, and I thought to myself, *"I have a good life."* I changed my mind about trying to search for them or to know them.

Time went on, and another year had passed. I had met several different young boys that I thought I would like, but I would ask myself, *"Suppose he is related to you biologically?"* I went to my mother again and asked her to make another appointment for me to talk with a social worker at the Children's Aid Society. She did. It was the summer of 1969, I was out of school for the summer and had graduated from Beaubien Junior High

School and was to start High School in the fall. I had finished two semesters at Vernor, and I went to a new Junior High school that was built for the students in the neighborhood. In 1967-1969, I went to what was then Beaubien Junior High on Wyoming Street.

My father took off work early that day, and we went to the Children's Aid Society. I was afraid. Maybe my biological parents don't want me to know or find them. Maybe they moved out of state, or maybe they gave me up for adoption because they didn't want any children. I was having a lot of different thoughts and still asking myself, do I really want to know who they are?

I went in with the social worker, and it was just she and I. I remember her telling me that I was one of the first minors who wanted to know about my biological parents. Most children "she said, do not want to know who their biological parents are, until later on in their adult life." Because my adoption was a closed adoption, she could not give me any identifying information. My mother voluntarily placed me for adoption. Both her and my father were very young and were African Americans. She gave me bits and pieces of information about my mother, but very little about my father. She told me the date and place where I was born and how much I weighed. I left there feeling somewhat satisfied with the information I received. One thing I left knowing was that they both were too young to take care of a child, but I believed I was born out of love.

A couple of days after my visit at the Children's Aid Society, my mother showed me the adoption papers from Probate Court that showed the process in which I was adopted. It was one particular paper that had the name that my biological mother had given me at birth. The name was **Jacqueline Elaine Dunbar**. Wow! I didn't think too much of it at the time when I saw it, except, "Huh, my adoptive mother changed my name." I always kept that birth name in the back of my mind. I found out later that the middle name Elaine is the middle name of my biological mother. After I found that out, I felt special and believed that she cared enough about me, to give me her middle name. They say, there is power behind a name.

The name Jacqueline is a beautiful name, which means, protected by God, the supplanter. Sigmund Freud has a quote that says: *"A human being's name is a principal component in his person, perhaps a piece of his soul."* When I think about the name change, I thought about how God changed the names of the people He called. He changed Abram's name to Abraham, Simon's name to Peter and Saul's name to Paul. There is power in the names. Because my name was changed, I believe it did not change my destiny of what God has for me. I like the name "June" given to me by my adoptive parents; it means youthful and freedom-loving. My adoptive mother told me that she named me June because so many wonderful things happened to her in the month of June. She was born in June, got married in June and she loved the TV show, Leave It to Beaver and named me after June Cleaver, the wife, and mother on the show. I figure the last name that I was given was taken from my biological mother's last name and would be a help in my search to find her.

As of this day, I still do not have a birth certificate, all I have is a certificate of registration from Lansing, Michigan with my adopted name, birthdate, address and my adoptive mother and father name.

Well, I was thankful that I had some information from the Children's Aid Society and the information my mother had shown me from the adoption papers answered some of my questions. I knew a little bit more about how and why I was adopted and also knew a little about my biological parents.

This started me to pray almost every night that God would bless me to find my biological family.

The fall of 1969 had come, and it was time to go back to school. I started at Henry Ford High School on Evergreen, in Detroit, and graduated in June 1973. I met more young people in High School that I didn't know in Junior High. Most of the young people that I went to school in junior high with went to a different high school than I did. It was my mother and father that had put in a transfer for me to go to Henry Ford High thinking I would have a better education. I did not want to go to Henry Ford; I wanted to go to high school with my friends that graduated with from junior high school. But I went away and didn't really like it. I started skipping school the first year and wasn't very focused on my education. I would go downtown or hang out at the malls until I finally got caught one day and my mother put me on punishment. After my first year at Henry Ford, I changed most of my classes to Business classes, and I was a little more focused on school, and I did well.

I became friends with some of the young people I met in high school. We hung out together. I would talk with a few of them I had gotten close to and told them about my adoption. Sometimes it would make me feel special when I talked about it. Knowing that I was handpicked, sometimes made me feel free, sometimes it made me feel that I didn't belong to my adopted family, and. I was just out here in the world not knowing where I came from. At times, it was such a lonely feeling, that I didn't want to get close with anyone really because we may have been related.

At the age of 15 years old, my mother started letting me go out on dates. It was mainly with the young men from church.

Friends That Are Family

I had a close family that I grew up with from our church whose house I would go over every weekend. Sometimes our mothers would say that I was not going over there that weekend, and as it ends up, I stayed at their house for the weekend, or she would come over to my house. Cheryl was like a sister to me. She had three brothers who were like my brothers, and their mother was another mother to me. Because there were more people at Cheryl's house, I always wanted to go over there. I had a lot of fun at their house, and they always made me feel welcome. We would play games, play the record player and listen to music, and dance. One thing I learned from being around them, was how to cook a hamburger. Cheryl's mother would let us make our own hamburgers. That was fun to me. I would talk with Cheryl, and her mother about my adoption and they would listen. They never really gave me any input on what to do as to trying to find my biological parents, but. they would just assure me of the wonderful adoptive parents I have and how they really loved me. When we would travel, and go out of town, my parents made sure that Cheryl would go along with us so I would have someone to keep me company. I became acquainted with Cheryl's families on both her parental and maternal sides. It is a coincidence that Cheryl has a first cousin on her paternal side, who was born the same day and year that I was and we found out that we both have the same blood type. To this day, we call ourselves twins. I think we were also born around the same time of the day; he said he was born at home, and I was born at Crittenton Hospital in Detroit, Michigan.

The question would continue to rise up within me again, *"Who do I belong to?"* or *"Who was I attached to for nine months?"*

I enjoyed being around families that were closely knitted. It gave me the help and support I could not seem to find in myself or my family. I did not understand that it was God's love assuring me that I was not alone. God put people in my path that showed me love, and I will be forever grateful for them. We all desperately need a sense of family, relationship, and belonging. God created us to be in families, which is an institution that God ordained. We have a natural hunger to be a part of something that gives us a sense of acceptance, affirmation being needed, and appreciated: especially adoptees. We want to belong, to connect, and feel connected.

In December of 1969, I was reacquainted with a young man that I had met some time before who was also from Detroit. We were at the

National Church of God Youth Convention in Rochester, New York. Every year during the Christmas Holidays, when the young people are out of school for the Christmas break, the Church of God has a youth convention where young people come together from all over the United States for Fellowship and Worship. Each year it is in a different state. The Services and workshops were from three to four days. I started going every year when I was around 11 years old. It was a lot of fun, but our counselors made sure we went to every service.

    I already knew of the young man because I went to elementary and junior high school with his cousin. One evening while in Rochester, New York, they had a skating party for the youth after service and I went along with a few others from Detroit. One young man that I knew from junior high school introduced me again to this young man. He was a very good skater. We skated together a couple of times, and I started to like him. He was a total gentleman. When the convention was over, and it was time to come home, all of us from Detroit came back on the train. He and I sat together on the train, and we talked and got to know each other a little better. We exchanged phone numbers, and he told me when we get home he would call me the next day, and he did. From that day on, we would talk every night, when we got home from school. He was working at that time, at a shoe store downtown, so I wait for his call when he got off work. When the new year of 1970 came in, we were at watch night service at my church, and he asked me "Will you go with me?" and I said "Yes!" The year 1970 was a good year for me. He asked me to be his girlfriend, and I felt very special. Every weekend he took me out and on Sunday's we both had to go to our own churches. In the afternoon, sometimes we would get together for a minute, and then he had to go back to his church for their youth meeting, and I had to go back to my church for our youth meeting). He was also brought up and raised in the Church of God. Some Sunday evenings he would leave his church early, and come over to our evening service. When he came, we would go out and get dessert at Howard Johnson's restaurant, or we would just come back to my house, play records or look at the TV.

Every time we would go out, he would take me to some of the very nice places, beside McDonald's and Burger King. This same year in 1970, it was an Easter Sunday and my girlfriend Cheryl met a young man from her school, and they had been talking. Cheryl went to Cass Tech high school, and so did her friend. Cheryl asked us if we would pick her and her friend up so we would all go out to dinner that Sunday, and we did. We picked up Cheryl's friend and went to the Mauna Loa restaurant. In that day, it was a very exclusive restaurant and had a beautiful décor of Hawaii. From then on, every weekend Cheryl and her friend, and Freddy and I would double date.

As the days went by, our relationship grew closer. I started talking to him about me being adopted, and one day I wanted to find my biological family. When I first start talking to him about my adoption, he just said that I looked a lot like my adoptive mother's side of the family and that it didn't really make a difference to him. He told me about how he was very close to his cousins that were adopted both of whom were around our age, so he knew a little about families that had adopted children. His cousin that adopted children always made sure when we would have our church gathering when the different churches would fellowship together, that my mother would see her children and that I would see her children and that I would see her. I guess the adoptive mothers would talk about their adopted children.

Now and then when he and I would go out or talk on the phone, I would bring up the subject of my adoption and that I wanted to know who my biological mother and father were. He would say that he believes I felt a genuine curiosity and believe that one day I would find them, but he would say he didn't know how I could do it.

In June of 1970, Freddy was graduating from Mumford High School (the high school I wanted to go to), and he asked me to go to the prom with him. I was so excited that I get to go to the prom with my boyfriend! My mother and I went shopping almost every day looking for prom dresses, shoes, and accessories. I didn't know what dress I wanted to get, so my mother had my aunt who was a seamstress to make me a dress. I end up having three dresses and still didn't know which one I was going to wear. I finally, at the last minute, made up my mind. I got my hair done. I had a lady to do my make-up, and I had all my accessories. The prom was over in Windsor, Canada at the Cleary Auditorium and it was lovely. Freddy was sharp, and we both looked good. I was still excited. When we got there, I saw a young lady with the same dress on that I had on. I was too through!

After all I went through trying to find a dress, and I had three brand new dresses, and I end up wearing the same dress one that someone else had. Then I didn't want to dance, or do anything, but sit in a corner. I had lost all my joy, but after time, I got it back, and we had a really good time. I wanted to make Freddy happy because it was his prom.

Cheryl and her friend graduated that same year, and their prom was the same night. So, after we left Freddy's prom we went and picked them up, and we hung out together all night. Cheryl's friend, Curtis Smith, is now her husband and they have been married over 40 years. \

Chapter Six

Help! I'm Trying to Find Myself

*"God is within her; she will not fall;
God will help her at break of day."*

Psalm 46:5 NIV

The year 1970 was coming to a close. Freddy and I had been going together almost one year. I was in love with him, and I believe he was in love with me. He had graduated from high school, and in the fall of 1970, he attended Highland Park Community College in Highland Park, Michigan. He was still working at Bakers Shoe store. I was in the 11th grade and was doing a little better in school. I was feeling pretty good about myself. My parents were providing me with what I needed and what I wanted.

At Christmas time, my parents signed me up for a driver training school for one of my Christmas gifts. So, when February 1971, came I would be 16 years old, and I would be ready to get my driver's license, but little did they know or probably they did know, when Freddy and I would go out on a date, he was teaching me how to drive. I could hardly wait until February 22, 1971, would come so that I would get my driver's license.

Because of me giving love, I felt I started to know what love is. This is when I begin to experience the unconditional love God gives to us. *"God's love has been poured into our hearts through the Holy Spirit that has been given to us."* – *Romans 5:5NIV.* This awareness of love started to linger within me and encouraged me to be loving. *"Above all, clothe yourselves with love, which binds everything together in perfect harmony."- Colossians 3:14,* God love is a powerful feeling. I think about the song that said: "Jesus went to Calvary to save a wretch like you and me, That's Love!"[1] As I began to feel the love that God has given me and how he gave his life for me, I started thinking more about my biological mother and father and had a more desperate urge to find them. I already had a feeling, that no matter what reason they gave me up for, I felt a love for them. I would imagine about the gift of love, what better gift could I give them, than the very love out of which I was created!

Freddy was a young man that was showing me a lot of affection, attention, and love and that is what I was looking for. What he was offering me, I accepted. We became a little too much involved with one another, and I became pregnant. *Oh, no! why did I get involved like that? My mother is going to kill me!* I tried my best to keep it hidden. I didn't know what to do. I started having morning sickness, and I missed a couple of days of school.

---

[1] Allen, David L. "No Greater Love." *Live at The Miami Civic Auditorium.* GWMA Mass Choir. Gospel Music Workshop of America, 1986. Vinyl recording.

Then around the middle of February, we had our semester break, so I was glad I didn't have to go to school. I stayed around the house being sick. I was trying to think of what to do to keep it from my mother. My mother and I never talked about this, but I know she knew what was going on. Abortion in those days was not legal here in Michigan., so that thought was out. Later, the United States Supreme Court ruling of January 22, 1973, (Roe vs. Wade and Doe vs. Bolton), struck down the laws in all 50 States, allowing abortion for any reason up to the moment of live birth. The father of the child (even if he is married to the mother), has no legal right to prevent the abortion.

I had heard of some of the things that young ladies would do to try to abort their babies, but I was too afraid. After a couple of weeks went by, I started feeling better, still knowing that I was pregnant. One thing I said, I was not going to do, was to give my baby up for adoption. I said whatever I had to go through to have the baby and keep it, I would do it and suffer the consequences. I told Freddy that I thought I was pregnant, he said "Let's make an appointment with the OB/GYN doctor and see what they say.' My mother always paid attention to my menstrual cycle. Finally, she asked me if I had my menstruation for the month? Of course, I lied and told her, "Yes." The next month came around, and she asked me again. This time she told me she was making an appointment for me to see an OB/GYN doctor. OH, BOY! The day of the appointment had come, and I was so nervous and afraid, but what could I do but go and let it happen. I believe my mother was just as nervous and afraid as me. My father took off work early to make sure that we got there. The doctor examined me and told me that I was pregnant. I was between 10-12 weeks along. The doctor told me the baby would be due around October 12, 1971. He explained to me about being pregnant and things I would go through and things I should and could not do. After he talked with me, then he said I'm going to call your mother in, and we will tell her. My mother came into the office and sat down, and the doctor told her I was about 10-12 weeks pregnant, my mother hollered and fell out of the chair. My father heard my mother holler, and he came into the room, and the doctor told him that I was pregnant. My father said he thought that's what it was. I felt like I was nothing. I was so ashamed that I had let my parents down. I knew I had disgraced the family. We made it back home, and my parents discussed things with me. They asked me if Freddy was the father and I told them, 'Yes." They also asked me did he know that I was pregnant, and I told them that I did tell him that I thought I was pregnant. and we were going to make an appointment with the doctor, but they had beat us to it. Being, the loving parents they were, they stood by me.

After coming home from the doctor's office, I thought about my biological mother all evening. Asking myself what did she have to go through, how did her mother feel? How did she feel? Was she close with her family? Many, many things went through my mind just thinking I am in the same situation she was, but she was two years younger than me, when she became pregnant. But did that really make any difference in the situation! No.

That evening after Freddy got off work, I called him and told him we went to the doctor's office and yes, I am pregnant. He hesitated on the phone for a minute, and then he said, "We're work something out." I asked him was he going to tell his mother and father that evening, he said "No," he would tell them in the morning.

Before I went to bed that night, I prayed and asked the Lord to forgive me and help me in this situation as we made decisions that would be best for the families. I also prayed for my biological mother, who still may have been going through some things in her life, that is affecting her today, because of her decision to give me up for adoption.

The next day was a Saturday, and Freddy's mother called my mother and said that when Freddy got off work, that they would like them to come over to our house and talk with us. My mother, of course, said "Yes." That evening Freddy's, brother, mother, and father came over. I was so scared of what they might say. We all sat down in our living room, and we all had some things to say. After much discussion, both families agreed that Freddy and I would be married. Freddy's brother was very much against us getting married, but it happened. On Tuesday, March 16, 1971, (I found out that March 16, is my biological mother's birthday), Freddy and I were married at my parents' home m. that evening. We had a few family members and friends to come. Because I was too young to sign for myself, my parents had to sign for me to get married. Freddy was old enough to sign for himself.

We were starting a new journey together. I was now a wife and soon to be a mother. Again, I thought a lot about my biological mother. I had to shift my way of thinking and doing things, now that I was a wife. I knew this was not the way life was supposed to go for me, but I trusted God to help me make the right decisions. All the while I was still praying that one day I would find my biological mother and father.

We lived with my parents after we were married, and they brought us a 1966 Mustang. Freddy loved cars and took good care of it. He was still working at Bakers Shoe store and going to Highland Park Community College. I stayed at home while I was pregnant, and was learning how to cook and be a wife. I finally got my driver's license after we were married. I was able to make all my doctor's appointments and take my mother and godmother around.

While I was pregnant, I would think about what I was going to do after the baby was born. For one, I knew I was going back to school and get my high school diploma; then I wanted to enroll at the Detroit College of Business or try to find a job. A couple of weeks before the baby came, my Uncle got Freddy a job at the Chrysler Glass Plant on Wyoming/McGraw in Detroit. We were all excited. In those days, it was who you knew that could get you a job at either General Motors, Ford, or Chrysler automotive plants. We called it "The Big Three." They had good pay and benefits. Freddy didn't mind working hard to support his family.

On Thursday, morning September 30, 1971, at 7:15 am, I gave birth to our son, Frederick Jamal, weighing 7 pounds & 2 ounces and 21 inches long. When Frederick was born, he had jaundice and had to stay in the hospital for two weeks. After five days, I came home and was very sad that I had to leave my baby at the hospital. I didn't know that I had the RH negative blood type and when mix with the RH positive it causes the baby to be Jaundice. I went back to the hospital every day until we were able to bring him home. Okay, now this is it at age 16 years old, I am now a wife and a mother. Wow! That was too young, but I did it. And I was still wondering, *"To whom do I belong?"*

Freddy and I were both blessed to have good parents that were very supportive and good to us. Freddy's parents always treated me like their daughter, instead of a daughter-in-law. My mother-in-law would remind me that before my adoptive mother passed, she asked her to be sure to take care and look out for June. After the baby came home, we all were very excited and started loving on him. We were blessed that after jaundice went away, he was a normal healthy baby.

In January 1972, when the new semester begins, I went back to Henry Ford High School Adult Education and completed all my classes and received my high school diploma in June of 1973. We thought things were going pretty good for us. Freddy was working at Chrysler and was going to school, I was at home with the baby during the day, and at night I went to school. When Freddy started working afternoons, he bought me a car, which was a Grand Torino.

We had been married for 1 year and 6months, when in September of 1972, Freddy received a letter from United States Army Services, stating he was drafted into the Army Services. We all were devastated! We thought since he was married, had a child and going to school that he would be deferred from being drafted. We started asking for help. We asked our pastors to write letters stating it would be a hardship on the family if he went into the service. We also asked some political leaders to write letters to get him deferred but to no avail. His parents, my parents, our friends and I were all upset that he had to go into the army. September 21, 1972, he had to be at the AFEES Induction Center at 6:00 a.m. I took him to the place where they had to enlist for duty. He got out of the car, with a few things that they told him to bring, I didn't get out the car, but watched him go in, and I said a prayer for him. I cried all the way back home. I didn't hear from him, until around two days later. He told me he was at Fort Knox, in Kentucky to do his basic training and would be there for about 6-8 weeks. Freddy got sick with pneumonia and stayed in Fort Knox for four more months. We all were praying for him that he would not have to go to Vietnam. Thank God, he didn't. He did his basic training at Fort Knox and then spent the rest of his time in Germany. One of the things that hurt so bad was that he had to go into the services eight days before our son's 1st birthday. I now had to take care my son on my own, but again, I had the help of my parents, and Freddy's parents were very supportive and helpful. Being there in the service for only two months, Freddy didn't have any leave time coming, so we all went to see him that November, for the Thanksgiving Holiday. In December of 1972, Freddy was able to have a furlough pass for two weeks. He came home for the Christmas holiday, and we had a wonderful Christmas that year. When he left to go back, of course, we were all sad again.

My first year of marriage as a wife and mother made me feel good about myself. I now had someone that belonged to and was a part of me, as I stated in chapter five, this is a natural hunger to be a part of a family or something that gives us a sense of acceptance, affirmation and being needed and appreciated.

In June of 1973, after I completed High School and received my diploma, I started working part-time as the Secretary for the Joseph Campau Church of God (the same church that I grew up in). The money I made from working, I bought gas for the car, paid my parents rent and a few personal things I needed. Freddy was sending me a monthly allotment, and I started a savings account, so when he came home, we would have enough for a down payment to buy a home.

In September 1974, Freddy received an honorable discharge from the U.S. Army services. Our entire family and friends were blessed that Freddy was returning home. Freddy was also blessed to have been working for Chrysler one year before he was drafted and was able to go back to work at the Glass Plant with no problems and his seniority was still intact.

When Freddy returned home from the service, we were making the adjustments and getting back to the routine of things. Our son at the time was three years old, and they had taken some time to bond and reconnected as father and son. Freddy missed two years of our son's life, from being in the service.

When Freddy went away to the service, it gave me time to become a little more mature and really look at life, because we married so young. Of course, he also came back more mature and knew how to take on responsibilities.

In October 1974, we started looking to buy a house. We were living with my parents, and my mother came to us one day, shortly after Freddy had come home, and told us we had until the end of 1974 to find us a place to live, so we started looking. We would get the paper every day and look up homes for sale. I had an uncle that worked for a real estate company, and he was working with us. The latter part of November we found one that we felt would fit our budget and we purchased it. We were now proud young homeowners, at the age of 19 and 21. We moved into our home on December 4, 1974, and I have been living in this same home for 42 years. For the next few months, we were enjoying being in our own home, working, and seeing our son grow up. I felt good that I had accomplished a family life. I have a son, husband and a home that was a part of me. But I still questioned myself, *"What is it that's missing?"*

The Spring of 1975, Freddy got sick. He couldn't keep anything on his stomach. He was losing weight and was very weak. He kept going to work, but he was still sick. He was laid off for a while, and this gave him a chance to seek medical help. He went to several different doctors. They could not diagnose just what type of sickness he had. Finally, he went to one doctor, and this doctor found his blood count was down too low and immediately rushed him to the hospital. They ran all kinds of tests on him until the doctor found him to have Pernicious Anemia. He stayed in the hospital for about two weeks. We continued in prayer for him, and slowly his blood count started coming back to normal. Pernicious Anemia is a condition in which the body does not have enough healthy red blood cells. Red blood provides oxygen to the body tissues. Pernicious Anemia is a decrease in red blood cells that occurs when the intestines cannot properly absorb vitamin B12. Pernicious Anemia is a type of vitamin B12 anemia. The body needs vitamin B12 to make red blood cells. You get this vitamin from eating foods such as meats, poultry, shellfish, eggs and dairy products. A special protein, called intrinsic factor (IF) helps your intestines absorb vitamin B12. This protein is released by cells in the stomach. When the stomach does not make enough intrinsic factor, the intestine cannot properly absorb vitamin B12. In adults, symptoms of Pernicious Anemia are usually not seen until after age 30. The average age diagnosis is age 60. When the doctor diagnosed what the sickness was, and explained to the family about it, we were surprised that Freddy had this condition at such a young age. To build his blood count back up, he had to have B12 shots, every week, then every other week, then once a month until finally every three months. Whenever his blood count was low, he had to go back to this same routine.

We had another rough episode in our marriage, which we had to make it though. Freddy was again away from the family, sick and in the hospital and I didn't know at the time what was going to happen. I was trying to get prepared to take care of a sick husband. I had always been depending on him.

After around 6 to 8 months later after Freddy's sickness, we were back to our normal routine. I was still working at the church; Freddy went back to work at the Glass Plant and was finishing his classes at Highland Park Community College and received his Associate Degree in Business Administration. Our son, Frederick II, was getting ready to start kindergarten in the fall of 1975.

In the fall of 1975, I became pregnant. We all were so excited about having another child. I didn't want my son to grow up as being the only child like me. For me, there was always a feeling of being lonely. I had said to myself after Freddy had gotten sick and our son was growing up, that if I could not have any more children, I thought about adoption for us. Thank God, I had a normal pregnancy. While pregnant with my second child and having to know a little more about life, the question came to my mind of my biological mother carrying me for nine months. *What were her thoughts in knowing that she was carrying a baby in her womb, that she would give birth and have to give the baby up for adoption?* I finally tried to understand my biological mother's perspective and grasp how hard her decision must have been.

I would talk with my adoptive mother about my pregnancy, and she would explain to me about her sister's experience of being pregnant, but she would say, "I'm sorry, I have never experienced being pregnant to know." This was one conversation I missed having with her, as a pregnant woman talking with my mother about pregnancy. But we would talk about everything else. She was a good listener and was someone I could always talk with.

I read an article in the Guideposts magazine that was titled "A Question of Motherhood, the only one who could understand what I was going through was the mother who gave me up." The story was about an adopted young lady that was pregnant with her first child. In her fourth month of pregnancy, she was experiencing stretch marks. She was on the bus one morning on her way to work, and she pulled out her phone and read about a new app and downloaded it, and it was based on the book *What to Expect When You're Expecting.* She said by this being her first child she was full of questions. As she was reading, she came to a section that stated: "If your mother got stretch marks, chances are you will too."

"My mother?" she thought. "Which one? There was Mom, who had raised me since she was two weeks old and then there was her birth mother."

Her mom that raised her had no experience with pregnancy and childbirth, but according to the app, the best person she was to get help from would be her birth mother. She had first met her birth mother when she was 19 years old. Her birth mother had reached out through the adoption agency years before to find her daughter to tell her that she had been diagnosed with cancer. The birth mother and daughter corresponded through letters for five years and finally decided to meet. After their first meeting, they started talking on the phone and e-mailing each other like distant girlfriends. She stated that she couldn't dismiss the questions she had about growing up as an adopted child.

Her adopted parent shared with her what they knew about her birth mother and father, and that they did not marry because neither one could provide a stable environment to raise her. In her story, she tells about one evening she and her husband were eating dinner when her husband noticed something was wrong. She was worried about calling her birth mother and asking her questions about her pregnancy. She finally called her, and her birth mother was glad to hear from her and from that time on, she would call her every week throughout her pregnancy. When she went into labor and was getting ready to have her baby, she said she couldn't help but think about her birth mother. The birth mother's cancer had worsened and reached a critical stage After her baby boy was born, they went to visit her birth mother in another state. She was near the end of her life but was able to hold her grandson, tears streaming from her eyes, two days after that the birth mother died.

After I read this story, I thought about what I was feeling and the questions that stirred up in me while I was pregnant. I believe they were the same feeling the young lady in the story was having, but I didn't get to meet or know my birth mother at that time.

I was praying that I would have a girl. On Friday, May 21, 1976. At 5:30 am. I gave birth to a girl, that weighed 8 pounds and 8 ounces and 21 inches long. I name her Camille Rachelle Aundra Purifoy. The middle two names were after her godsisters, Rachelle and Aundra Freeman. I was ecstatic, Camille was a healthy and normal girl. I am blessed now to have a boy and girl.

When I was pregnant with my son and daughter, and I was going to the doctor each month for my prenatal visits, the doctor would ask me questions about my mother and father. What type of health problems or diseases that ran in the families? Were they smokers? Were they heavy alcohol drinkers? All these questions, I had to answer with I don't know, I was adopted. It is still like that to this day. If I go for a medical testing or see a new doctor for the first time, they will ask me the same questions about my family medical background. This was another reason why I wanted to find my biological parents.

After Camille was born, I didn't go back to work at the church; I stayed at home to care for my family.

I had high hopes for our family especially our children. I prayed that they would grow up and be responsible, respectable and God-fearing individuals. My prayer also was that we would be a close-knit family, who could conquer anything together.

What I knew for sure was that I had a family, that we were physically and spiritually connected. But, I still desired to know who I was connected to, by blood.

I have heard many ministers speak on the subject: *"You are not an Accident" Before I formed you in the womb, I knew you"* from Jeremiah 1:5 NIV. As an adoptee, you don't feel like that. You feel as if you were an accident and someone felt sorry for you and knew you needed some help. In his book, *The Purpose Driven Life – What on Earth am I Here For? Written by Rick Warren,* he brings out some good points, referring to "you are not an accident." He stated before the universe was created, God had you in mind, and he planned you for his purposes. These purposes will extend far beyond the few years you will spend on earth. You were made to last forever! The meaning and purpose of your life by looking within yourself is the wrong place to start. He stated you must begin with God, your Creator, and his reasons for creating you. You were made by God and for God, and until you understand that, life will never make sense. After reading his book, it helped put a little light on the subject, for me. As I start getting older and more mature, I know I was created by God, and He breathed His life into me and sent me through my mother for my life purpose. So, I had the assurance during this time of my life that I was going to be able to find and meet my biological mother and father.

Chapter Seven

Damaged Goods
***"Surely goodness and mercy shall follow me
all the days of my life:"***
Psalm 23:6 KJV

As an adoptee, I sometimes have felt like damaged goods. I heard another adoptee say the same thing. He made mention of a dog being in a shelter, and someone finally came and gave the dog a home. Some animals have been abused and neglected by their family and left out in the streets; the humane society will come and pick them up, bathe them, take care of them and place them for adoption. As he stated, we have more animals being adopted than children.

I have felt at times, like the damage items in the groceries store and the clearance items in the retail stores. In each of the stores that have the damaged items they usually have a certain section in the store for just those items. In the grocery store, if you see damaged items with the rest of the items that are on the shelves, they will take it out. Or if you see that dented item in the midst of the good items, you can ask if you can have that one for a discounted price. If no one buys these items, the stores will end up giving them to local food banks or charitable organizations, or some may be thrown away. I have felt that I was on a shelf, waiting to be picked by someone, still in good condition, but my damage was given up by my biological parent.

Then there was starting to be damage to my marriage. As time went on, a couple of months after my daughter was born, Freddy and I started having marital problems. Many different incidents started to happen, but this one particular incident really was a blow to me. It was a Sunday, and the Chrysler plant where Freddy worked was having a picnic for all the plant employees at Edgewater Amusement Park on W. 7 Mile Road in Detroit. The amusement park has since closed, and it is now the Greater Grace Temple Church, where I am a member. The area that was a hurting field for me has now become a healing field. Freddy and my son went to the picnic. I stayed at home and was getting my daughter and me ready for another engagement we were invited to that afternoon over my cousin's house. Freddy was supposed to be back home around 3:00 pm to pick up my daughter and me. We waited, waited, waited until around 5:00 pm and he still didn't show up. I had one of my neighbors take me to the park to look for him. We walked around the park looking for him, and I didn't see him. I finally saw my son. He was with his cousin. I asked him where his dad was? He said he thought he was on the roller coaster. I went over there close to the roller coaster ride, and that's when I saw Freddy coming down the ramp, holding hands with a young lady that was his mother's neighbor daughter. My heart dropped to my knees! I said, what is this? Freddy answered me and said, "I brought her along to be with me." I could hardly see straight. I gave my daughter to my neighbor to hold because I didn't know what I was going to do. I was so mad! I started cussing them out, and I felt like someone had stabbed me in the heart and left the knife in me and kept turning it. I was so hurt. The young lady had someone else to take her home. I got my daughter and went and found my son in the park, and Freddy took us over to my cousin's house. I just started crying and told my cousin and family what had happened. He just sat there and didn't say anything much, except he was sorry, and there was nothing to that relationship. I wanted to believe him, but I knew it was a lie.

I believe that relationship between Freddy and that young lady went on for a couple of years, but they tried to keep it discreet and quiet. The worst part about it was that Freddy kept going on as if he didn't do anything. He still was providing for us and taking care of the household. When I would talk with my adoptive mother and father about the way things were going in our marriage, they would tell me to try and stick and stay, as long as he was taking care of all the bills and providing a home and food for the family, try to stay and work it out. They kept saying "You need your husband and the children need their father to help raise them." At this time. I thought about my biological mother and father. I had the feeling of being abandoned by them, now by my husband. But one person cannot work a marriage out by themselves; it takes the two to work together. We tried to stay together and work things out.

In 1977, I decided to search for a job, to help with the household budget and have some extra for my children. I got a job working as a Clerk-Typist at Michigan Wisconsin Pipeline, which was a part of Michigan Consolidated Gas Co. My daughter was one-year-old, and my son was five years old, and he had started school. I had a hard time trying to find a babysitter for my daughter because my mother and father-in-law were both working and my mother and father were sickly and couldn't properly care for her. The Child Care Centers only took children who were 2 ½ and potty trained. After working at Michigan Wisconsin Pipeline for almost two years, I decided to quit that job and try to find another job that was closer to home. When I was working for the pipeline, it was in downtown Detroit. It took almost 45 minutes for me to get to work, and if the traffic was backed up, sometimes it took almost an hour for me to get home. I wanted to spend time with my children during the day because they were very important to me. In the fall of 1979, I found a job at the Northland Nursing Center as a Nurse's Assistant working the midnight shift. I found that it worked out good for me because it was right down the street from my house and I could be at home with my children during the day. I would take my son to school and pick him up, and I finally got my daughter trained to the potty. I worked at the Northland Center from 1979 to 1985.

My son, Freddy was now 13 years old and my daughter, Camille was eight years old. They were able to have a key to the house and could come in the house after school. My son, when he was 11 years old had a paper route after school, which he had until he was 14. (he had a good route with good customers) the paper route taught him how to interact with people and how to manage money. He was also active in the school band from 4th grade until he completed high school. My son loved music. My daughter was active in tap and ballet, and she took piano lessons but wasn't interested in none of the above. My daughter when she was about 12 years old, would get with her girlfriends and they found interest in styling and doing hair.

Freddy and I were still having marital problems. When I thought, things were going well; something else would happen. I still didn't trust him, but we were trying to make our marriage work.

After six years of working for the Northland Nursing Center, I wanted to find a better job, working during the day. My children were older, and I could trust them to come home after school, stay out of trouble, and do their chores, so I was comfortable with the idea of working later hours.

In 1985, I found a job at the Comprehensive Psychiatric Services, P.C as a Collection/Medical Biller Clerk. I enjoyed that job because it was 10 minutes from my house. I started work at 12:00 Noon to 8:00 p.m. Of all the many jobs that I had, I always wondered would or did I come in contact with any of my biological family.

In 1988, I had to quit working for the Psychiatric Services and take care of my adoptive mother and father. My father was a blister diabetic, and he had started having fainting spells when his sugar count would be high and then go down too low. We could not get his sugar level stable. He would go in and out of the hospitals, and therefore he couldn't take care of my mother. I had to go over to their house every day and give him his insulin shots and make sure he had eaten properly. My mother had severe arthritis and congestive heart failure. It seems after my father got sick and his health was failing, she started giving up on life. She stayed in bed all day and only sat up to eat and go to the bathroom.

Finding the Missing Pieces

As my children were growing up and getting older, the desire to find my biological family grew too. My son started driving and had an interest in dating. His very outgoing personality led him to meet many different young people and doing a lot of traveling with his school band and the churches. My daughter wasn't as outgoing as my son, but she found enjoyment in being with her girlfriends. I know they were talking and meeting up with boys.

I started thinking about almost the same things for them as I did when I was young. *I wonder if they would meet up with anyone who is related to them from my biological mother or father?* I talked to them about my adoption and how I did when I became close friends to a male or female. But of course, my children not thinking like me, said, "Oh mom, you probably will never find your biological family."

Around the year of 1987, I made an appointment to see a social worker where I was adopted from at the Children's Aid Society. I believed that this time since I was an adult adoptee that was married and had two children, I would get more information. When I met with the case manager, she gave me a little more information than when I went at 13. She stated that consent was not on file in Lansing, Michigan, so identifying information could be shared at this time. The non-identifying information she gave me was the date I was born, the time, where I was born, how much I weighed, and how many inches I was. She did tell me that I was a healthy baby and very little information on the medical history of my biological mother or father. She also told me that they both are African Americans and their religious background was the Methodist faith. My biological mother was age 14 years old, and my biological father was 16 years old. My mother graduated from high school and enrolled in a junior college. My father graduated from high school too, but they did not have any more information about him. My mother is 5'5" tall, weighs 130lbs. has black hair, brown eyes, and light brown skin. She is a very pretty young lady with a pleasant manner. The worker stated that my mother voluntarily placed me for adoption.

Well, after I left the Children's Aid Society, I had a few more pieces to the puzzle in my mind. Month after month, I tried to put the pieces I had together and continued to pray. I shared the information I had with Freddy and my children, and they suggested that I still continued to look for them. I always reminded myself that they are not looking for me, so I shouldn't be surprised if I find them that they don't want to meet me. And that is one of the things the worker at Children's Aid Society kept reminding me. If my mother or father was looking for me, all they had to do was to write to Lansing, Michigan, and state they are trying to find me, which they had not done.

I started my quest. I knew what my mother's last name was at that time and what high school she and my father had graduated from.

In the summer of 1988, my family and I had joined a church that was located on the east side of Detroit. The Pastor of the church had married Freddy and me, and we were very fond of him. I knew several of the members there from previous churches we had attended over the past years. One Sunday a young lady whom I have known, came up to me and asked me if I was still looking to find my biological parents. I told her yes! The young lady told me that she worked at the high school where my mother and father had graduated. I gave her the information I had about both my mother and the little information I had about my father, and she told me she would see what she could find and let me know. During this time, I wasn't working, and I would go over to my parent's house every day to take care of them. For every caregiver that is a job within itself.

The young lady that worked at the high school called me about four weeks after she and I had talked about me finding them. She told me she had some information for me that I would find interesting. I asked her to bring it to church on Sunday, and she did. I took the information and looked at it again and again. I thought this might be my biological mother. Ok, I kept thinking to myself, *"Now that I have this information, what was I going to do with it."* Again, I was praying and asking God to lead and guide me on what I should do.

The information I had was on a 5x7 index card it had, the young girl's name, address, telephone number, her birthdate, her mother's name, her step-father's name and the date she entered the high school. The most interesting information was that she left school on 2-9-1955 under doctor's certification and re-entered school on 4-7-1955. Put two and two together which equals four. I was born on 2-22-1955 and six weeks after I was born was around 4-7-1955 was the time when she re-entered school. What I felt with this information was very important. It might be my biological mother.

Between this information, I had from the high school she attended and the information I had from Children's Aid Society, it looks like the pieces were coming together.

One day in August of 1988, my girlfriend Jackie had come by my house. We sat around and talked. I asked her to take a ride with me, and she said "Yes." I didn't tell her at first where we were going. I live on the Northwest side of town, and we were going on the east side, which was about a twenty to thirty-minute drive. As we were getting closer, I kept thinking to myself to turn around and go back home. This was an address from over 30 years ago, and they have probably moved and no longer live there. But, I went on, and I told Jackie what I was going to be looking for. I told her I was a little afraid to look for the house because they may still be living there or they may have moved, plus I didn't know what to say or what to do. She told me to go ahead and let's try to find the house, and if anyone is outside around the house, we'll tell them who we are looking for. If nobody is around the outside, I told her we'll just drive around; we are not going to get out the car and knock on the door. Oh, no! My friend Jackie is very outgoing and outspoken person, so I knew if we saw anyone outside of the house, that she would do the talking. She kept encouraging me to go ahead, and we continued to look.

As we rode around, we spotted the house and there just happened to be a man in the driveway working on a car. We slowly drove up and looked at the house to make sure the address was the same address I had from the index card, and it was. We drove by the house and looked again at the man in the driveway, and turned around and went by the house again. Jackie told me after the third time, to turn around and go back and she would ask the man if he knew the person that we were trying to find. I turned around and backed up and was at the end of the driveway. Jackie kept telling me she would do the talking. I said okay. Jackie hollered to the man, and he looked up and started walking down the driveway toward my car. The closer the man got to my car, Jackie commented about how he walked and looked like my son. When the man reached my car on the passenger side, where she was sitting, Jackie didn't say anything. She became speechless. (That was not like her). She then looked over at me and said, "June." I had to think quick and try to put some questions together to ask him. I said we are looking for, I gave him the young lady's name that was on the index card, and he said, "That's my sister! Why are you looking for her, she moved out of Michigan in 1963?" I kept saying "Uh, uh, uh," I couldn't think of anything to tell him why we were looking for her. I finally said we're her friends and tell her that June came by to see her.

OH, BOY, after we drove off all kind of thoughts and emotions were going on inside of me. Jackie kept telling me how my son looked and walked like the man who was so shocking to her that she couldn't say anything. It was an exciting day.

After I got home, Jackie and I kept talking about it. I told Freddy about what we had done. I told him that might have been my uncle. Freddy and I talked about it, and he said he had a curious thought of knowing who my biological mother and father are. He felt that I had a right to know, but again remember, that I am looking for them and they are not looking for me, so don't be surprised at what I might find.

Now the question was, what was I going to do from this point? I had another piece of the puzzle to put together, but it is still not completed. I was thinking about what the social worker and Freddy had said about me trying to find them, and they may not be looking for me. That was one of the things I wanted to find out for myself, were they looking to find me?

I didn't talk with many of my friends or family about this. I just kept praying and asking God for direction and what would be the next step to take.

Chapter Eight

Rejection Can Be Direction

*"As I look back on my life, I realize that every time,
I thought I was being rejected, from something good,
I was actually being re-directed to something better."*

Steve Marabodi

My curiosity started rising as more pieces of the puzzle came together.

Four to six weeks passed, and I was thinking about the day I went to the house and saw the young man. Of course, I didn't hear anything from him because I didn't give him any information about me, but I did get his name, and I still was holding onto this index card. One day I thought about writing a letter to the young man. I had his name and address, and maybe he would pass this letter on to his sister. So, I did. I wrote a letter explaining who I was and who I believed his sister was to me. I must have written that one letter 6 or more times, trying to think what to say and what not to say. After, maybe the 8th time in writing, I mailed the letter. I put my telephone number on the letter in case he wanted to call me, and I asked him if, after reading the letter, he would send it to his sister.

I waited a couple of weeks, and I didn't hear anything from him. After the fourth week, I decided to call him. I used the telephone number on the index card, and it was the right number. The conversation didn't go well; he didn't believe what I wrote in the letter and asked me what was I really up to? I was honest in what I was saying, and I told him why I was looking for her. The young man told me to "let it go, let the past be the past and bury it." After we finished the conversation, I hung up the telephone and started thinking; *I better give up this search.* As he stated, "It happened in the past. Bury it." Many days after the conversation with the young man the trap of fear set in. What if I found my biological mother and she does not want to meet me, and asks, "Why are you looking for me? I gave you up because I didn't want you." Many different thoughts of fear were going through my mind.

I had to decide to step out on faith or let fear convince me to shrink back. Each piece of information I had was bringing me closer to finding her. I felt I had come too far to stop now.

At the age of 33, I thought and prayed about this even more. *I know who I am* and *whose I am and that God created me for a specific purpose and plan. I believe that I know what my identity is in Christ and that He has a purpose and plan for my life, nothing can stop it. I have wonderful adoptive parents who care for and nurture me and have laid a good foundation for me.*

I chose to put my trust in the Lord, no matter how I was feeling or what others may think or do. I took a step of faith, knowing God was on my side and that He was for me. I prayed and asked God again to lead and guide me in the right direction to find my biological mother and father.

Answered Prayer

One Sunday after service was over, I went and spoke to the Pastor of the Church where I was attending, and I told him about what I experienced in the last couple of months while trying to find my biological mother and father. He stated he understood how I felt and would do whatever he could to help me. He suggested that after our church service was over, that he and I would go over to the house where we saw the young man, and he would see if he would talk with us. The Pastor told me when I was ready to let him know. Four weeks passed, and I called the Pastor during the week and asked him if he was available the following Sunday after church, and he said, "Yes." All that week I was thinking about what I was going to say or should I just let the Pastor talk. That Sunday, I went to church by myself, and I kept thinking about what I was going to say. I was really nervous. My Pastor asked me did I still want to do this? I said, "Yes."

After service was over, I left my car at the church and rode with him. He kept asking me was I alright, and we talked a little about why I wanted to find them. We got to the house, and we got out of the car and walked to the front door. I was so nervous. We rang the doorbell, and an older gentleman came to the door. My Pastor introduced himself and told the man my name and who I was. We asked for the young man that I had met that day when I drove by the house. The gentlemen told us that he was not at home at the time, but would be back home later. The gentlemen asked us to come in and have a seat. I got all choked up and could hardly say anything. My Pastor took the conversation over and told the man why we were there. He started telling the man about my family and me and gave a little background of my adoptive parents. The Pastor gave the gentlemen the young lady's name we had and asked him, "Was she his daughter?" The gentlemen said, "Yes, that is my step-daughter." The Pastor went on to tell him that I was looking for her just to know who she is and a little about her, and where I come from. He told the gentlemen that we believed that his step-daughter was my biological mother and that I was not looking for her for a handout or anything else. The gentlemen kept shaking his head, and saying, "No, I don't believe this is the right family you're looking for." My Pastor said, "Ok," but the gentlemen didn't say too much after that. We both left the gentlemen our names and telephone numbers in case anyone wanted to get in touch with us.

After we left the house, the Pastor told me that he believed that I had found the right family and the gentlemen just didn't want to say too much, without talking with the young lady first. The Pastor told me that I probably get a telephone call in the next few days. He dropped me off at the church to pick up my car, and I went on my way feeling like another weight had lifted off of me. I stopped by my adoptive parent's home to check on them. I hadn't yet said anything to them about what I had done.

When I got home that evening, my friend, Jackie, that went with me the first time over to the house was at my house waiting for me to come home so I could tell her about what happened that day. While we were talking, the telephone rang. It was the Pastor. He asked me if I had just got home and I told him yes. He told me that a lady was trying to call me, that had already called him, and he told me it might be my aunt. He told me he was going to hang up and be listening out for a call. Sure enough, about 15 to 20 minutes later, the telephone rang, and it was a lady asking to speak with me. I answered, "This is June." She asked me did I go by her stepfather's home today with my Pastor? I told her, "Yes." She asked me a few more questions, and I answered them. She told me she was the sister of the lady I was trying to find. We talked for a little while longer. She said she would call her sister, who lived out of state, and give her my name and telephone number and have her to call me. I was so excited; I didn't know what to say.

It was happening so fast, that I was just overwhelmed. I didn't think the family would respond the same day. I thought maybe they could get in touch with me in a couple of days.

About an hour later my telephone rang again, and it was the lady that I believed to be my biological mother. We talked for about an hour. She asked me some questions, and I asked her some questions. All the answers to my questions were mostly what I had thought about for the last few years. Thank You, God! I felt like the song, by artist R. Kelly who said, "I believe

I can fly, I believe I can touch the sky."[2] All the answers I had gotten from her, for the next several days I started putting them together.

For the next several weeks, the lady that I believed was my biological mother, and I continued to talk on the telephone exchanging information.

I prayed again, and asked God, "Is this lady that I have been talking to my biological mother?" He spoke softly to me and said, "Yes, this is your biological mother."

The information she gave me and the information I had received from the Children's Aid Society was the same. The high school and junior college where she had attended were the same. After I found her, I wrote to Lansing, Michigan. again, requesting information to make sure I had found the right family. But again, because she hadn't sent in a consent or a release to give out any information, they still would not give me their names or any more information than I already had.

She told me the name of my biological father and told me she believed that he still lived in Michigan. She didn't know any more information about him, just what she knew almost 35 years ago. She stated she hadn't seen him anymore after she left Michigan, which was in 1963.

A couple of months after we started talking, she told me that she would be coming to Michigan to see her family and to meet me. I was so happy that my prayers had been answered. I was telling everybody I knew, (except my

---

[2] Kelly, R. "I Believe I Can Fly." *I Believe I Can Fly*. R. Kelly. R. Kelly, 1996. CD.

adoptive parents) that my biological mother was coming to Detroit to meet me. Freddy and the rest of my family were also excited for me.

In the meantime, I would get the phone book and look for the name that she gave me of my biological father. I found several people with the same name. Again, I started praying and asking God to direct me to the right one with that name. One day, I got up enough nerve to call one of the phone numbers, and when someone answered the phone, I couldn't think of what to say; so, I hung the phone up. (Thank God, we didn't have caller ID and *69 and all the technology we have now). The next day I tried it again, I called that same number, and a lady answered the phone. I made up something to ask her, and she stated she didn't know what I was talking about and I must have the wrong phone number. When I hung up, I felt like a fool. I left that alone for a while and focused on meeting my biological mother.

Before she came, I got to meet her sister, which is my aunt and her children and grandchild who are my cousins. Wow! Things started moving pretty fast, and I finally got to meet some of my biological family.

One of my co-workers brings me a copy every day from a meditation from the Hazelden Series, "Each Day – A New Beginning"- illustration by David Syphon-Winston/Hazelden copyright @1982. This one meditation that really spoke to me was:

> *"No prayer goes unanswered. Of this we can be certain. The answer may not be what we'd hoped for, in fact, we may not recognize it as the answer. However, our prayers are answered, our problems find solutions, our worries are*

eased, if we but attune ourselves to the messages. They are all around. Be attentive to all the signs from God. Whatever answer we seek is finding its way to us."

A Special Time

The day came that my biological mother and her husband came to Michigan. They came to my home. When I saw her, I was in awe, because she and her family look so much like my adoptive mother's family. We sat and talked for a while, but it was like I was in a dream. I was on cloud nine. I showed her some pictures of me when I was a baby and as I was growing up. She told me you look like your father, especially around the eyes, she made that statement more than once.

Freddy waited around the house until they came to meet her, before going to work. He was excited for me too, that I finally got to meet with my biological mother. My daughter was also at home when she came, and she also got a chance to meet her. My daughter had mixed emotions, and she said she wondered if she would accept us like family. My son wasn't home; I don't remember if he had band practice or what, so he didn't get to meet her that day.

It was a day I will never forget. The visit went well, and she stayed around two to three hours. I took a couple of pictures of her, still in a dream that my biological mother came to see me. Even when she left, I was still in awe. She told me she was going to come back the next day and she did. So, my son had a chance to meet her, and he said, he thought to himself that he had another Grandmother. Those two days for me were unbelievable. My prayers were being answered. For the two days, when visiting with her, I felt an assurance that this was my mother.

After I woke up from my dream, it was then time for me to tell my adoptive parents what was going on. They both had been sickly and not getting out the house, except to go to the doctor's office, and my adoptive father was going in and out of the hospital. We could not get control of his diabetes, and my adoptive mother was suffering from severe arthritis and heart trouble. I began going over to their house at least twice a day to make sure they had their meals and had taken their medication and do some other things that were needed. I didn't know quite how to tell them that I had found my biological mother, but I wanted them to know before someone else tried to tell them. When I told my adoptive mother that I had found my biological mother and that she came to visit me, she didn't say too much. Maybe she felt that this would never happen, even though she used to tell me, anytime I wanted to look for them she would help me. I really don't know how she felt.

When I told my adoptive father that I had found my biological mother, he said, "This was a bad time to find them." I think the reason why he said that was because, at this time, they needed so much of my attention. Finding my biological mother did not or would not take away the love that I have for my adoptive parents. They were my parents that raised me and did all they could for me. I would never have forsaken them. I was still willing to do all I could to make sure they were taken care of.

After my biological mother left and went back home, we would talk on the telephone almost once a week. I had the pleasure of meeting with some of her other family members. I met a special couple that was my biological mother's aunt and uncle with whom I became friendly. I would go to their house and visit with them a lot. The aunt had severe arthritis, but she was able to tell me a lot about the family history. I took it all in. I really enjoyed spending time with her and her husband. This aunt had only had one daughter, and she lived in California with her family. I was glad I had a chance to meet her too. She would come here to Michigan to see her mother and father, until a year or two later; the daughter moved her parents to California to better take care of them. I sure did miss them. My biological mother's sister showed me much acceptance. She would come and take me around to meet the family members here in the city, and I became close with her son and daughter-in-law, which are my first cousins. I was enjoying meeting all the family. My biological mother's sister wrote a book about their Grandmother, entitled "Remembering Granny" a novel by Gloria Dunbar. It tells of the life of their grandmother growing up as a country girl in Georgia and later in life moving to Detroit, Michigan with her family. I was able to glean from her book which gave me more information about the family and the lady who was my great-grandmother.

That following year in January 1989, my adoptive father died from complications of diabetes, which was really difficult time for my adoptive mother and me. I thought my adoptive mother would pass before my father because for years, she was always sick. During this time, I had to think about my adoptive mother and how I was going to take care of her and so many things. This was a time in life when I had to make some decisions for which I was not prepared. I had to do some praying and asking God what was best for my adoptive mother now. I wanted to move my family in my adoptive mother's house, so we could better take care of her, plus her house was bigger than mine. When I talked to Freddy about it, I told him we could move in with my mother, and we could put our house up for rent. No, he said, I could move in with my mother, but he was staying in his house. This was a complicated decision; do I move in with my mother or stay in my house with my family? My son and daughter were both a big help to me. They would stay with my mother during the week and some weekends too. I also had friends that would go to my mother's house and help me in taking care of her.

One day, my adoptive mother became very sick and started having chest pain. We rushed her to the hospital, and she had congestive heart failure. She stayed in the hospital around two to three weeks. When I was visiting with her, she told me to go ahead and sell the house and put her in a nursing home. I did not want to do that; I wanted to continue to take care of her. I knew it would be a bit much trying to take care of her and my family at home, but I felt I could do it.

I went on and did as she asked me. We found a nice nursing home facility in the city that some of our church members had their family members there, which made it good because she always had someone to visit with her. My adoptive mother was pretty content with being there. The first day we took her and signed her in, I cried all the way back home. It really hurt me to think that I couldn't take care of this lady who took care of me from when I was ten days old.

After selling my parent's home and getting all their business straightened out, I took a trip with my friend Sheila, to visit another friend and to visit with my biological mother. After I was born, my biological mother had another daughter five years later. She told me she had never told her daughter about that she had another child, until after I had found her. I was also planning on meeting her other daughter too. When we arrived at my friend's house, I called my mother to tell her I was in town. She came the following day to my friend's house and picked me up. We went out to a restaurant and had lunch. The other daughter came and met us there. I was so excited that I got a chance to meet my sister. She introduced me to her. We ate and talked for a while; then she had to leave. My biological mother and I stayed at the restaurant and continued to talk. I know this was a shock for her and I don't believe she accepted me. That was the first and only time I saw her and had a conversation with her. I know this was a hard pill for her to swallow. She took me back to my friend's house, and I was glad to see and spend some time with her again.

As we were traveling back home, I was thinking a lot about her other daughter and their relationship. Like Freddy would tell me, this is what I wanted, was to find them. They may not have felt the same way I did about me finding them. I have to respect each individual's reaction if this is not what they want.

The Search is On

After I had met my biological mother and her family, the search was on again to find my biological father. I searched in the telephone directory again, and it was the same list of people that I found the first time I looked. (Too bad I didn't have the internet or ancestry.com back then to do the searching). When I talked with my biological mother, I asked her different questions about my father. One thing I remember her telling me was that she thought their family was in some type of construction business. After looking through the directory, one name stood out for me, and that was the name and telephone number I tried before. One day I got up enough nerve and called the number again. A man answered the phone, and I asked to speak with (I gave the gentleman's name), and he said, "This is he." When he said that it was him, I got so nervous that I broke out in a sweat. This time I had written out a speech on what I was going to say and ask. I pulled out the paper I had and begin to talk about my biological mother. I asked him if he knew or remembered her and he said, "Yes, I know her." I said, "She told me she used to be your girlfriend." I went on to ask if he went to the same high school and a few more questions. Then I told him that my biological mother told me that you are my biological father. He hesitated for a minute and then said, "Yeah!" He told me a few things about what happened and how he heard that I was given up for adoption. I told him a little about myself, and he kept saying, "This is how fate would have it." We both agreed that we wanted to meet each other. I told him where I lived and he told me where he lived. I made mention to him that he lived close by the church I attended. We made a plan that the following Sunday after church, I would come to his house and meet him and his family. This time was also exciting for me. What I had been praying and dreaming about it was coming to pass. After we got off the phone, I told my family that Sunday after church, we were going to meet my biological father at his home. I was telling my friends about how excited I was to go and meet with my father and his family. I got different comments from some friends that said I should be careful. "Maybe you all need to meet for the first time at a mall or restaurant" they warned me. I said," No, I'll be okay." It seemed it took so long before Sunday came, that I could hardly wait. At church that Sunday, I couldn't focus on the service, for thinking *"Today, I was going to meet my biological father."*

When service was over my son, my daughter and myself went over to the house. (Freddy didn't go with us, he had to work). We were greeted well by the man I believed was my father. We sat down, and we talked, and I was amazed that I looked like him, especially around the eyes, just like my biological mother and her sister had said. I was also amazed to be there in his home. After we were there for a while, his father, which was my biological grandfather, came by. He came over to meet my family and me. I was so glad I had a chance to meet him too. The grandfather was nice to me, and we exchanged phone numbers. My father's wife stayed in the kitchen and didn't come out or sit down with us. I felt a little uneasy about that and felt she didn't want us over there. My father told me he had four sons but always wanted a girl. He didn't tell me the names of his sons and I didn't ask. I didn't get a chance to meet any of his sons that day. We stayed for about an hour and left. This was another wonderful day for me. Now I had met my biological mother and father. Thank you, God!

My biological father told me that he really didn't have any say so on how things went when my mother got pregnant; because he was so young, he didn't have the means to take care of a baby. The same way things happened for my mother; she was very young and could not take care of a baby. Her mother did all the planning and preparation for her. My father said after my mother became pregnant, he was not allowed to see or talk to her. My father's parents were asked to take me, but they had just had a son that is about two years older than me, and they didn't want to take care of another baby.

After the first visit with my father, I made several phone calls to him, but he did not call me back. I started thinking about the visit and the phone calls I was making and thought to myself that they didn't want to be bothered. I had a talk with my father's parents a couple of times on the phone, and my family visited with them at their home, but I could feel that they were putting up a wall between us and I could only go so far.

After a couple of months had passed, I finally talked on the phone with my father, and he told me his wife could not accept me in his life. I felt hurt, of course, but I remembered that I wanted to find them, they were not looking for me. A couple of weeks after I spoken with my father, I went over to my father's parents' house to talk with them, and we talked about the same thing, that my father's wife did not accept the way I was coming into his life. I said to myself: *I will not call or try to see them again.*

Years went by, and I didn't talk with or see my biological father or anyone in his family. But I kept believing that I didn't find them for naught. I know God still had a plan and purpose for me as to why he let me find both of my biological parents and their families and in due time it will be revealed. I wasn't going to give them up.

Chapter Nine

Connected by Grace

***"My grace is sufficient for thee;
For my strength is made perfect in weakness."***
II Corinthians 12:9 KJV

The next couple of years by 1990-1992, and I only talked with my biological mother, maybe once to twice a year. Maybe I would get a Christmas card from her. I believe she felt the same way my father and his family felt, so I didn't pursue any further relationship with her. I'm glad I took some pictures of her when she came to visit with me that I could always have as a keepsake. I did feel content that now I knew both of my biological parents, a little about their lives, their families, and why I was given up for adoption.

My prayers were answered. I had found them. I continue to trust God, knowing that God's design for the family is always to be a place of love and acceptance.

My adoptive mother was still in the nursing home and was doing pretty well. I focused a lot of my attention on her. I would visit with her 3 or 4 times a week, still taking her out to the mall, taking her for lunch or dinner and sometimes she would come home with me and spend the whole day with my family and me. The early part of 1992, she had a slight stroke, and she didn't feel like doing much of anything but stayed in bed. Later that year on December 16, 1992, two weeks before Christmas my adoptive mother died. The time after her death was a hard and lonely time for me. When making the arrangements for her funeral, I felt like I was in this world all by myself. My son had graduated high school, and he was busy working, into his music, and taking classes at a Recording Institute. My daughter was still in high school, and she was working and hanging out with her friends. And Freddy was always working. When I was going to make the arrangements, I went myself. My adoptive mother's family turned away from me and didn't keep in touch with me after they heard I had found my biological parents. One of her family members told me, I didn't need to find them. My adoptive mother never asked me any questions about my biological parents, and I didn't say anything about them to her.

Life goes on. I have found that everyone has experienced some lonely times in their life, even if sometimes their immediate family is close around. These are the times when you're by yourself and wonder *"Why am I here?"* I had to put the question inside of me, aside, and just keep it moving and continue to trust God for my destiny and plan He has for me.

I always wanted to call my biological mother and father to see how they were doing and just to say hi, but I didn't. I kept telling myself you found them and know who they are, don't bother them. I began to wonder again, *"Did I find the right parents?"*

In the early 1990's I started doing Day Care in my home for about four years which brought me much joy. One of the babies I cared for was my first cousin's son, which was on my biological mother's side of the family. Caring for him brought a closeness to me as being a part of the family. I told his father and mother how I appreciated them for letting me keep him. It gave me the feeling of a connection with my natural family.

I started keeping my Goddaughter when she was around three months old. I became very attached to her, and I was believed that maybe this was my purpose in life: to take care of children. I had many children that I care for and loved.

After the children grew up and started pre-school, I had to start thinking of something else to do.

In my neighborhood, there was a Salvation Army Denby Children's Center, that I had driven by many times. I always thought about the children that were in the center and thought about doing some volunteer work there. At the Church where I was attending, I was the President of the Women's Ministry, and I was looking for an outreach program that we could get involved with to do some volunteer services. I talked with the women at the church, and one of our women told me she did volunteer services with the Bible Study program with the children and she enjoyed it. We took a census to see how many would be interested and I had them to sign-up. I got in touch with the Captain and Director of the center, and he told me, "Yes," they needed some more volunteers to assist with the Bible Studies. I brought it back to the women of the church, and they agreed to do it. We all had to take a TB test and have a police clearance done. We were excited about serving with the children. I served in the maternity program, where young girls between the ages of 12-18 were there during the duration of their pregnancies. They were wards of the Court. The mothers and fathers had lost their parental rights. The girls were pregnant, and the majority of them didn't want to stay in foster care while they were pregnant. The Captain's wife was over the maternity program, and I started doing the bible studies with her. We had to clock in at the time clock before we started. One evening I saw a job posting for a part-time Receptionist. I thought this would be a good position for me to apply. I filled out an application and got the job. The Salvation Army Denby Center was a center for abused and neglected children who were taken away from their parents. It was very interesting to me because I saw how the foster care system worked with Child Protective Services, the Courts and the different state children agencies that were involved.

I worked as a receptionist at the front desk for about one year; then I had to take a medical leave. I thought I was going to be off work for about six weeks, but it ended up being five months. I had a complication after my surgery. By me being on leave so long the Center had to hire someone else for that position. When I finally return to work, they offered me a better position as a full-time Secretary in the Maternity social services department. I accepted the offer and was very thankful to get it. One thing I can say about the Salvation Army is they were a good organization to work for and looked out for their employees. This time I had the chance to work directly with the teenage girls that were pregnant. The majority of the teens wanted to have their babies and keep them. A few started out in their early trimester thinking about giving their baby up for adoption, but those thoughts were usually changed after six months or more. This also gave me a feel for how it was with my biological mother. She told me when she was pregnant with me, that she was in a place for young ladies who were pregnant. My heart went out to these teenagers. Working with these teen girls every day, I thought a lot about my biological mother. My biological father told me how he wanted to go visit with my biological mother when she was in the home, but he was not allowed to visit or call her.

Knowing I could have been in the same situation, being a 16 years old pregnant teenager. I'm thankful I had good parents and good in-laws that were very supportive of me. The teen girls were just like any typical teenager that was interested in boys, liked dressing up, keeping their hairstyle, and some liked to dance and party. But one thing all of them desired was to be loved and to belong and connected to a family. I knew this feeling very well. Most of the teen girls wanted to keep their babies with them and not have the baby go in one foster care home, while they went into another one. They didn't want to be separated from their babies. They wanted to show that they could be responsible and mature mothers that would take care of their babies and for the state to find them places where they could live independently. The job of the social workers at Denby was to monitor the teen girls during their pregnancy and see if they were capable of living independently or if they needed to be placed in foster care. We had to prepare reports for the 60, 90, and 120 days on each girl, and send it to the state showing how they were doing in school and around the

Center. A few of the girls had already had a child; this was their second pregnancy. Their first child may have been with relatives or in foster care. I felt a lot of the feelings these teens girls were going through, wanting to keep their babies because this is one of the only things that belong to them, that they could love and the child would love them back. When I became pregnant with my son, I felt that this is a human being that is a part of me, blood connects us.

While working at the Denby Center, I saw one incident that hurt me to my heart. I cried almost all day long for this young mother. The young mother got into an argument with a pregnant teen. She already had her baby and had come back to Denby until her worker could find her placement. The baby was one-month old and was a very pretty baby girl. The mother was holding the baby when she was arguing and threw the baby at another teen girl to hold, while she was fussing and cussing. One of the social workers saw this happen and because of the protection of the baby, they had to call Child Protective Services, who came out to the Center and took the baby away. The young mother was hollering and crying. It was the saddest situation I saw while I was working there. The young mother left a couple of days after that, and I don't know where she went or if she got the baby back. The staff didn't talk about it. A lot of different things happened while I was working there and I could see myself and what may have happened with my biological mother. I worked for the Denby Center for six years, and I know it was not by happenstance, it was the divine order of God, that I was employed there. The Denby Center later became a shelter for families, and in 2015 the Center closed its doors.

On January 16, 1998, my daughter, Camille had my first grandchild who was a boy, Jamal Raymone Mitchell. Jamal brought plenty of joy and happiness to the family; we were so excited when he was born. What made me so happy, was that I was there in the hospital room with my daughter when she started having labor pains and was there throughout the delivery. She was only in labor for about 3 hours. Then to see that new life coming into the world was amazing. I was a proud grandmother that cut the umbilical cord. After Camille and Jamal came home, Jamal has done nothing but bring joy to my life. I was so grateful for the Denby Center, for they were very supportive of Camille and Jamal by showering them with all kind of baby items, so much so that the first three months after Jamal was born, Camille didn't have to buy anything. What a blessing they were.

I wanted to call my biological mother and share with her, about the good news that she was now a great-grandmother, but I didn't because I didn't know how she would receive it. It's many things that were happening in my life that I wanted to share with her, but I felt uneasy and chose not to bother her.

I Held on to My Faith

Many different things had happened over the past years in my marriage that totally destroyed it. Freddy had started staying out all night and weekends. When he did come home, he said he was working a lot of overtime. I tried to get back at him by doing something I just couldn't do for the sake of my children. He would find time to come home and get the household bills and pay them, but I always wondered, who else's bills were he paying! He had stopped going to church because he claimed always to be working. Finally, he didn't come home for one week, two weeks, and then three weeks and then he got some of his clothes and moved out.

In 1997, Freddy and I were divorced. We had been married for 26 years, and during those years it was a fight. I tried to hold on, but he wanted to let it go. I am very thankful for all the people that supported me during this journey in my life. Again, it was a time when I wanted to call my biological mother and talk to her about what I was going through, but I didn't. My adoptive parents had both passed away, and again I felt alone and hurt. But I was thankful for the Denby Center and the Greenfield Church of God, Pastor Michael Coleman, the members, and my friends who were very good supporters to me when I had to go through the divorce process. Because of their support and prayers, I was able to make it through. I had a very special couple who literally took me by the hand and helped my family and me, that was Deacon Rensely & Elsie Morrow. Elsie Morrow passed away on Christmas Day, December 25, 2012. Deacon Morrow is a man of great wisdom, and I remember him telling me after they had helped me along, that "it was time for me to grow up." I had always been depending on someone else, and it was now time for me to stand on my own feet. Divorce is a very painful experience. It was a very deep hurt. Over the years, the wound had healed. Freddy became one of my good friends.

In 2000, there was a job opportunity open for an Administrative Assistant at the L.I.F.T. Women's Resource Center, located in Oak Grove AME Church, in Detroit. The L.I.F.T. (Lifting in Faith Together) Center was a non-profit organization that services women in substance abuse recovery programs, domestic violence, women in the community, and homeless shelters. The L.I.F.T. Center provides women with life skills workshops series called the Positive Change Project. They also provided: Parenting, Computer Employability Training, After Care Support Group and a Clothing Boutique. The Center was birthed from a ministry with a rich legacy rooted in improving the quality of life for African Americans. The same spirit moved and compelled the Founder/Director, Rev. Dr. Jessica Kendall Ingram in 1990, to launch a ministry to women in the community.

My daughter's god sister told me about the position and suggested that I apply. She was on the Board of Directors; I figured if I applied, she would help me get the job. So, I thought and prayed about it, and I went and applied and got the job. I really didn't want to leave the Denby Center, but L.I.F.T. was offering more money which I needed now that I had to take care of things on my own. I believed it was time for me to leave the Denby Center. I put in my two weeks' notice at Denby and started working at the L.I.F.T. Center in May of 2000. We had a staff of only five ladies, and we worked well together. The L.I.F.T. Center not only serviced the ladies that would come for the workshops, but it took me to another level as a woman. All the different facilitators that would come to the Center to do the workshops provided good information and resources that helped to build my self-esteem and self-sufficiency.

While working at the L.I.F.T. Center, the Board of Directors hired a strategic planner, named Matthew Parker who was the President and founder of the Institute for Black Family Development. Mr. Parker came to L.I.F.T. to help the organization grow and to succeed. Mr. Parker also was working with the staff and gave each one of us an initiative to pursue. He taught us how to develop and do grant proposals. Mr. Parker would ask me about going back to school. I thought about it several times and would say, maybe later. He came to me one day and asked if I would be interested in coming to a meeting he had to get a group together that would like to attend William Tyndale Bible College. Again, I thought about it, and I went to the meeting. It was a group of people there that wanted to further their education, and he had staff there from the college to explain about the program, to answer questions we had and if we were interested, in setting up financial assistance with us. It was about 15-20 people that sign up and said they were interested. I was one. I enrolled. The plan was to earn an Associate Degree in Leadership within the next two years, but after the first semester, for some reason, the college closed up. But, Mr. Parker didn't let us down he kept encouraging us, and he started a certificate program called the School of Management for the group, under the Institute for Black Family Development. After we completed the certificate program, The Institute for Black Family Development partnered with the Great Lake Christian College, where the main campus is in Lansing, Michigan. Our group hung in there together with the help of Mr. Parker and in 2009, I graduated from Great Lakes Christian College with an Associate Degree in Family Life Education. All the teaching and instructions I had with Mr. Parker taught me a lot about families. This was all in line with what my focus is all about, family. So again, I would think about my adoptive and biological families.

One thing about Mr. Parker, he is a man of God and a man that is true to his word. He is now my mentor.

I loved working for the non-profit organizations. The work is so rewarding, especially when you are helping people and seeing the results of their needs being met. When I worked at the Denby Center with the pregnant teens, most of them had problems and issues with their families. For various reasons, they were removed from their parents, or their parents may have put them out of the house and given up their parental rights when they became pregnant. Some of the teen girls did have visits on the weekends from their mother or father or a relative. Some didn't have anyone to visit with them. When I was working at L.I.F.T., I interacted with some of the mothers whose daughters were at the Denby Center. It was very interesting again, for me, but I know it was in God's plan that I got to see and work with the Mothers and their daughters. It really gave me a clearer picture of what a mother goes through when she has to give up her child; and what a child goes through when they have been given up and are in the foster care system. Both the mother and child have hurt feelings. I see how it was the same with my biological mother. She was in the Florence Crittenton Home for unwed pregnant women, when she was pregnant with me. I believe we both still have some hurts from this situation.

The Florence Crittenton Home was a home devoted to caring for unwed pregnant women from their teens to their mid-20's, who stayed in one wing of the home during their last days, weeks, or months of their pregnancy. The young women were cut off from family and friends and faced with one of the hardest decision of their lives, to place their infant for adoption. My biological mother was a resident there in 1955.

The home was located on Woodrow Wilson in Detroit and was built and opened in 1954. It was in conjunction with the Crittenton General Hospital. They say it was a service tunnel that connected the hospital to the home. The home closed in 1974 and is now Cass Community Social Services, and the hospital moved to Rochester, Michigan and is Crittenton Hospital Medical Center.

What Happened?

One day in October of 2011, we had a meeting with the President of the Board of Directors, the Executive Director and the staff at L.I.F.T. In the meeting, we were informed that the Center had to let the staff go, because of a lack of funding. We were so upset when they gave us only two weeks' notice to clean out our desk and our office. What was I going to do? We were too through! We knew they were having funding problems, but we did not think it was going to come to this. In 2006, they cut our hours to only five hours a day and never brought us back to full-time, which was eight hours per day. But we still kept our health insurance, which was the main benefit I needed and we continued to work. I knew I would apply for unemployment and I was glad that L.I.F.T. had paid into the unemployment compensation, despite being a non-profit organization. Since most non-profits do not pay into unemployment compensation, their employees cannot collect unemployment if they are let go. I had worked for L.I.F.T, for 11 years and had planned to retire from there. I wondered who was going to hire me at this late stage in my life. Thankfully, when I applied for my unemployment benefits, I received them.

At the unemployment office where I had signed up, they had a club for those that were seeking employment that were 55 and over called the 55 Plus Club. I joined the club, and we met twice a month and discussed how hard it was to find employment for people our age. The workers at the unemployment office would help us with our resumes, our interviewing skills and at each meeting give us some job leads. Members of the 55 Plus Club, through Michigan Works, was offering Club members the opportunity, to go back to school if they wanted. They would pay for tuition and books, and you could select the school of your choice. I took advantage of the opportunity and went to Wayne County Community College and took classes for a certificate program for Case Management. After the completion, I received a certificate.

Chapter Ten

I'm God's Responsibility

"For ye have not received the spirit of bondage again to fear; But ye have received the Spirit of adoption, whereby we cry, Abba, Father"

Romans 8:15 KJV

I still wanted to talk with someone besides the Board of Directors, about seeing if they could get us back to working at L.I.F.T. They still were open and were having workshops! I guess it was not meant for me to go back.

A thought came to my mind to talk with First Lady Crisette Ellis, who is the first lady of my church, Greater Grace Temple in Detroit, where Bishop Charles H. Ellis, is the Senior Pastor.

In January of 2005, I was looking for a church home. I said I was going to start the new year off by visiting different churches and see where the Lord would have me to go. One Sunday, I got up and at first, I said, I was going to stay home because it was very cold and we had a few inches of snow. I said no; I got up and got ready and thought to myself, *I'll go to*

Greater Grace Temple today. It is only a few blocks from my home, so I didn't have to drive far and practically around the corner. I made it a few minutes late. When I got there, the service was on fire. For it to be a cold and snowy day, the church was full of people. I saw a few people that I knew, and I enjoyed the service very much. The following Sunday, I said to myself, *I think I'll go back to Greater Grace this Sunday*, and from that Sunday on, I went to Greater Grace every Sunday and never visited any other churches. I prayed about it and asked the Lord is this where I am to worship? A couple of months later, I became a member. I joined in the new member's class that they have for those that join the church, and I met a lady in the class name Deborah Starr-Hodges, who worked for the Capuchin Soup Kitchen. Deborah and I became good friends. Deborah had come to L.I.F.T., to facilitate a workshop and to tell the ladies about the services that Capuchins offer. My grandson and Deborah's son were in a mentoring program at the church, so we saw each other frequently. I would talk with Deborah about some of the things I was going through at L.I.F.T. After they let us go, I was really disgusted.

After what had happened to me at L.I.F.T. I said I was going to talk with First Lady Crisette Ellis. First Lady was a big supporter of the L.I.F.T. Center. She came and facilitated some of the workshops and events, sponsored L.I.F.T.'s Picnic, and she was always giving to the women. And plus, first lady and Rev. Jessica Ingram, the founder of L.I.F.T. were friends. I made an appointment with the first lady, and we met, and she really encouraged me. We didn't even talk about her talking with Rev. Jessica about getting me back to L.I.F.T., but she went in another direction and told me perhaps it may be time for me to leave L.I.F.T. She encouraged me so much and told me how I was "God's Responsibility," and that He would look out and care for me. She told me to keep my confidence in God, and He would see me through. I left there feeling good, and I had confidence in God that I was going to make it.

Maybe it was a month later, after our Sunday service, Deborah came to me and asked if I was still looking for a job? And I told her," Yes." She told me she could help me. I was glad for her to make the offer. I applied for many different jobs but was never called for an interview, so when she asked me about a job, I jumped on it. She had received a new position at her job, and her old position was open. She told me to bring in my resume and cover letter to her, and she would give it to her supervisor and put in a good word for me. I did as she asked. A couple of days later her supervisor called me in for an interview. The job position was for an Emergency Assistant Intake Worker at the Capuchin Soup Kitchen's Service Center. I went to the interview and met with the supervisor of that department and the director of Human Resources. The Capuchin Soup Kitchen impacts the lives of hundreds of people in Detroit on a daily basis. Founded in 1929 by Capuchin friars and the Secular Franciscans, the Capuchin Soup Kitchen is rooted in the Franciscan tradition of feeding and nourishing not only the body but the soul and spirit as well. The Service Center distributes 13,500 pounds of food each day to approximately 170 families and/individuals. Also, the people are welcome to get clothing items and other household items that are donated. As it was another non-profit organization, I believed it would work out well for me. The interview went well, and they offered me the job, and I accepted. My first day on the job was February 7, 2012. My position is to interview the guest to find out what are their needs are and set up a file for them and service them according to how many people are in their household.

After I worked for about two weeks, I questioned myself? *Why did I accept this job*? It's further than I had to drive to work in the last 25 years. I have to use more gas for my car, and I am not making the hourly wage that I should be making along with a few other things. But I kept going every day, because I loved working with the people and interacting with them, not to mention that we have a great bible study and prayer on Wednesdays, led by Bro. Jerry Smith, the Executive Director that gave us a lift for the day and week.

Believe It or Not!

After I had been working there for about a month, I was working at the front desk answering the phones when a gentleman came into the center. When I looked up at him, I said to myself, *Boy, does he look like my son*. He came and signed-in and had a seat. I went back to my desk and saw he was on my schedule. I called him in, and I made arrangements for him to get what he needed, and we had a general conversation. Something inside of me kept jumping around, it wasn't a nervous feeling, but it felt like butterflies were moving inside of me. I had a thought that maybe the young man might be my brother. He had the same last name of my biological father, and I remembered that my father told me that he had four sons, whom I never had a chance to meet, and I only met my father one time. After he left my office, I kept thinking about him all day. I asked the receptionist at the front desk, that make our appointments for our schedule, that whenever this gentleman comes in, (and I gave her his name) please put him on my schedule. I thought about this gentleman a lot and how much he looked like my son.

A couple of months went by, and I was at work ready to begin my day. I looked at my schedule, and to my surprise, this gentleman's name was on my schedule. I will never forget that day it was August 28, 2012. I wondered to myself, *Ok, what questions was I going to ask him? Should I say anything about the father or should I just ask him questions about himself?* I was writing down some of the things down that I wanted to ask. He came in for his appointment on time. I called him into my office and asked him to have a seat. I updated his information in the system and was getting a little nervous about what to ask. I started with a few questions about his father and mother. (I guess he thought, why is she asking me this). He answered them with what I had expected him to say, then I asked, 'Did they ever talk about a lady named June? He hesitated for a moment and said: "You're my sister." I said, "Yes, I believe so." We hugged. For me, knowing I had just met my brother was like the floodgates of heaven had opened and joy bells were ringing, and I felt so happy. I went around telling all my co-workers, "That's my brother!" After he left out of my office, he went and called his mother and told her what had happened. He came back in my office and brought me his phone and said, "My mother wants to talk with you. At first, I said," No," because I didn't know whether or not she was still upset. But I got on the phone, and she explained to me that what happened to her and the family that made her upset and she said that she is now over it and that we will have to get together. I felt so relieved when I talked to her and couldn't wait until the day when we would get together so I could meet the rest of my brothers. It had been 24 years since I had met with my biological father, and that day was the first time I met one of my brother's.

Family Connection

From that day on, I have been on cloud nine knowing that I finally have that family connection. What I had been praying for and more had come to pass. In my prayers and thoughts, I didn't really ask God about finding my siblings; it was more about wanting to find my mother and father. All the pieces have come together, and the dots have been connected. Now, not only did I find my biological mother and father, but I have four brothers from another mother and one sister from another mister. I got a chance to meet another brother when I was at work, the first brother I met, which was the third oldest, brought the second oldest brother to meet me.

Thanksgiving and Christmas Holidays were coming up, and we talked about getting together. For the Thanksgiving holiday. I would cook and have my mother and father-in-law over and a few other friends. Our family is a small family, but I always did love to have a family get together. We had the Thanksgiving dinner over to Freddy's house. I invited my father and his wife and my brothers. My father and his wife weren't able to come, but the brother I had already met came along with the oldest brother, which was my first time meeting him. We sat and talked and they told me some things about their father and the family. All of my father's family that I met would say how much I resembled my father's mother. I enjoyed having them over, and I could have gone on and on that day, talking to them and asking questions about the family. Each one that I had met, I felt a closeness to. I don't know if it's because woman attracted to a man or what, but around them, I did feel a welcoming. I had one more brother to meet, and that was the baby brother.

My father's wife told me she always had the Christmas dinner; then she invited my family and me to come. I felt really special again that on Christmas day of 2012 I was going to be with my biological father and the family. I could not have asked for a better gift than what I received that day. I think, even my son and daughter were excited about spending that time with the family.

That Christmas day, we made sure we started our day to visit with my in-laws first, and then we went over to my father's house. I felt that welcomed again when we walked in the door. There were more family members and friends over and everyone there was saying the same thing, how much I resembled my father's mother. It made me feel so good to now know who I looked like. My biological mother and her sister both told me that I look like my father, but that was before I had met him. And my father looks like his mother.

Words cannot explain how I felt that day, with being around my blood family. All I knew, was that I felt great satisfaction, relief, peace, and a part of a family. I have also met two uncles, cousins, nieces and nephews. I am so happy for a relationship with my biological family. We get together for the holidays and other special occasions.

I had to go and tell First Lady Crisette what the Lord had done for me. She spoke into my life and told me I was God's responsibility, and He would take care of me. I didn't know that God was going to work things out where I would get re-acquainted with my father and meet the rest of the family. I told her the story, and she got excited for me and suggested that I write a book about it. This is how it started. She had me to give my testimony to the Powerful Women of Purpose to encourage other women to not give up on trusting and believing God for what you have been praying for, and He will come through. I started praying about finding my biological parents when I was 12 years old.

Confirmation came for me in 2014, for me to write this book. We had our Powerful Women of Purpose Boot Camp 5, and it was dynamic. The Powerful Women of Purpose is the women's ministry at Greater Grace Temple, started by our First Lady Crisette Ellis, who is the Director. It is a very phenomenal and inspiring conference where we, as women, come together and are empowered to move up higher and grow deeper in God. We had some awesome speakers at Boot Camp 5, that empowered us to "Stir Up the Gift." That was the theme for that year. We had a luncheon, and all the speakers were on a panel, where we had a discussion and could ask questions. One of the speakers told us about how she had been journaling and from her journaling she had written a book. That was confirmation for me. I have been journaling since 1997 which has been a healing process for me, and it was spoken that day to me, to write.

There is a movie I love to watch entitled: "Somebody's Child" It is a story of hope, forgiveness, adoption and how things can turn in your favor. The beginning of the movie starts out when a teenage girl is in the hospital, and she gives birth to fraternal twin boys. She couldn't keep both of the babies but had to give one up for adoption. The adoptive parents who were going to adopt one of the baby boys were right there at the hospital ready to take the baby and raise as their own son. The baby boy she gave up had a birthmark on his shoulder, and before giving him up, she kept looking at it so that she could always remember it.

As the movie went on, 37 years later the teenage girl was a woman who had a kidney disease and was on dialysis. She would go to the hospital to have her dialysis treatment, and by her going often, she would see this young man who was doing janitorial work at the hospital. When the son she raised came and picked her up from the hospital one day, she asked her son to speak with the young man about doing work at his restaurant. The family had a restaurant that they owned, and the son was the manager over it. So, her son talked with the young man and asked him if he would be interested in doing work at the restaurant. He gave the young man his business card, and the young man said, "Yes, I'm interest. I will come by." The mother was glad that her son spoke with the young man and they went on their way. The next part shows where the young man goes to the restaurant and meet with the mother's son. The son was interviewing the young man and found out a little about his background. He told him that he had been adopted, but his adoptive parents divorced and neither one of them wanted to keep him. The young man had lost his hope after his adoptive parents placed him back in foster care. He had become very bitter and angry about his life. He said he went from place to place. As he grew up, he still had that bitterness and anger. He said one day as he was driving, he had a lot on his mind and he had an accident and ran his car into a couple and the accident killed the couple. He was charged with manslaughter and went to prison. He had been released from prison a few months and was living in a half-way house, trying to get his life together. The son had finished interviewing him and told him he was hired. After he had been working at the restaurant for a while, he asked the son for some time off. He said he had some important business he had to take care of. In the meantime, the doctor's office called the mother and the son to tell them that they had a kidney donor for her. She and her son were very happy to hear the news. The mother was going to the hospital to have her kidney transplant when at the same time the young man had taken off work for some business. Come to find out that the young man gave the mother one of his kidneys. The son found out that the young man had donated his kidney to his mother and he went to him and asked him, Why did he do that? He said, he really didn't know why he did it, but he felt it was the right thing to do since he was a match for a kidney for the mother. He also said the mother was so nice and good to him. The mother really started to like the young man, and she invited him over to her house for dinner. The mother and the young man were talking, and the young man told the mother how he appreciated the invitation to come over and how she was a nice lady. He also was telling the mother a little about his background and stated he had been abandoned twice, once by his birth mother and the second time by his adoptive mother. He didn't know his birth mother and father, but he knew he was "somebody's child."

While she was preparing the dinner, the young man had something to drink, and the dog came in the house and was running through the house and accidentally jumped on the young man and made him spill his drink all over his shirt. The mother saw what happen and came running in the dining room where the young man was and told him to take off his shirt, and she would wash it. When he took off his shirt, she notices that the young man had a birthmark on his shoulder, that resembled the same birthmark that was on the baby boy's shoulder that she had given up for adoption. She fainted! But, she knew right away that the young man was the son she gave up. She was calling her friends to let them know, that son she gave up for adoption she has found. Nearing the end of the movie is when the mother gets very sick, and they had to rush her to the hospital. While in the hospital, the young man came to visit her and she told him all about what had happened and that she was his biological mother. She said she had also written a letter to the other son to read when she had found out that he was her son. The mother asked the young man to please forgive her for giving him up for adoption. She felt she was dying. The young man told the son what their mother had told him and the son couldn't believe it. After 37 years, he found out he had a twin brother, and it was the young man who was working with him at his restaurant. The son stated he thought it was a coincidence that when he hired the young man and entered his information into the payroll system, that on his ID they had the same birthday. In the end, the mother died, and the brothers bonded together and started a close relationship with one another.

What my life and this movie demonstrate is, that when you are an adoptee somehow in your lifetime, your paths will cross with your biological family, whether you know it or not. I believe when I lived in my old neighborhood, I crossed paths with my biological parents; but I didn't know them then. Later after meeting them, I discovered that we even had the same likes and dislikes.

The movie also illustrates that the mother had a connection to that young man, while he was working in the hospital, which made her ask her son to ask him about a job. There was a feeling there, even though she nor the young man knew each other. The connection we have with those in our bloodline can be amazing. And if love is there, love will find a way! So much in this movie reveals the powerful tools of forgiveness and love.

God Word tells us in Jeremiah 1:5 *"That when you were in your mother's womb, He knew you."*

Chapter Eleven

Complete in Him

"And ye are Complete in Him, which is the head of All principality and power."
Colossians 2:10 KJV

Through Prayer, Patience, Trust and Faith in God are a winning combination for life. I now have complete knowledge of my genealogical roots.

I loved my adoptive parents very much and appreciated how they were preparing me at an early age, emotionally about being adopted. They used the teddy bears, talking with me through various stages of my childhood about my adoption, showing me the paperwork of the legal procedures, taking me to Children's Aid Society to let me talk with a social worker and they did many other things to prepare me. My adoptive parents were very open with me on discussing my adoption, and when I would ask them many questions, they would answer. But, at the end of the day, I don't think anyone really understands what adoption feel like, except the birth mother and the child. As a child when I thought about adoption, I thought about a mother giving her baby away to a couple that desperately wanted a child. Now, as an adult and having children of my own, I see adoption as a traumatic separation between a mother and her child. I believe that the birth mother struggles with the feeling of giving up her baby. The child does not experience this feeling when they are a baby or a toddler, but as the child grows up and goes into adolescence, they begin to have the feeling of abandonment.

This is why when people want to adopt a child, they want to adopt a newborn baby. With a newborn baby, they can raise and lay the foundation of their family structure for the child in the way that they are living; which is one reason why there are so many children in foster care that are predominantly older, that people don't want to adopt. The older children may have emotional, physical or mental disabilities and some of the children have special needs. Older children who have spent many years in foster care have a great need for adoptive parents. These children have experienced problems and emotional trauma, including being separated from their families and siblings. While in foster care some have experienced sexual abuse, and some have lived in foster care homes where drugs, alcoholism, and violence were prevalent.

My daughter-in-law, Geralyn, is an Intake/Assessment Worker, at a psychiatric hospital that provides inpatient psychiatric treatment for children, teens, and adults with mental health disorders. The majority of the children and teens that are patients are those who have been adopted, in foster care, or wards of the court. Most of the children have been abused sexually, physically and mentality, which has caused these mental disorders. The children that are 13 and under are still growing, and they can't usually pinpoint the diagnosis for the child. Some children cannot articulate and tell what is going on with them. They act out and therefore have these behavioral issues. (Then we have people that have adopted children from other countries, who have problems with the children, and end up in the hospital with mental disorders). Hopefully, if they get the necessary treatment and love they will grow out of these issues, but some of it follows them into their adulthood. The teenagers who are 13 and older, have started becoming aware of what has happened to them. As the old folks use to say, "they start smelling themselves." They question who they are, why am I here and they have problems with emotional behaviors. She told me how it's really a problem for the teen who has been adopted by a couple with the same sex. They are teased by their peers a lot and can't take it. This is why the bible states, *"Train up a child in the way he should go: and when he is old, he will not depart from it."* Proverbs 22:6. This is for all children.

I know of a single woman that was in the process of adopting a young girl (between the age of 10-12). She had so much trouble with the girl because the girl had mental issues that she gave the young girl back to the children's agency. The agency placed the girl back into the foster care system. Sadly, the young lady gave up and didn't try to adopt another child.

Children that are in foster care and adoptees today have access to receive treatment from a therapist to help them cope with being in foster care or being adopted. Also, adoptees have support groups they can go to if they need it. My support group has always been the church where I attend. When I was growing up, most African Americans did not believe in going to therapists or psychiatrists. We tried to handle our problems and struggles ourselves. My adoptive parents believed in prayer and counseling with their pastor. I do believe that my adoptive parents tried to educate themselves on issues related to adoption before and after I was adopted.

What was I in Search of?

I was in search of love and connection. One of my favorite songs that answers many of my questions is a sung by, Bebe Winans. I love this song!

Searching for Love (It's Real)

Searching for love…
Has anyone found it?
You see everyone knows
That love is a feeling.
But I know it's real
So, let my record show
And everyone here knows that it's real.

Searching for love…
Some search for a lifetime
It hurts and I know
To look for and don't find.
Can't smile until my record shows,
And everyone here knows that it's real.

(Searching for, looking for, nothing less, nothing more)

So how can I prove what I'm saying
When it's the heart that is filled with such joy?
The words that I say express the way that I feel.
It's more than just a feeling
It's the reality of this whole world:

Love in the form of a babe that was born to reveal.

Searching for love…
Some search high and low.
Which is the reason why I sing
To tell those who don't know.
There's no rest until my record shows
And everyone here knows that it's real.

What he is singing about is the love of God, because when you have found that love, it lets you know who you are and whose you are. This is what I found in all of my searchings, the love that God has given to me.

When I was a little girl growing up and being the only child, I couldn't understand my identity and experiences as to why I felt like I did. I was in search of someone to play with, someone to talk with, and someone just to be around. Sometimes as I got a little older, I felt like a castaway, out here all by myself. That was when I always had my teddy bear always with me. It gave me comfort and security, something that I could hold on to and say it was mine.

I had material things, toys, bikes, clothes and other things I needed and wanted. My adoptive parents provided the best things for me and the love they could give me, but we didn't have that bloodline connection. I felt something was missing.

Coming into my adolescence years, I searched for connection in friends, but that didn't work because what I wanted and was feeling, they couldn't give me. That is when I started gravitating to boys, not only would they say they liked me, but they gave me attention.

I know we were too young, but the one thing that I loved about Freddy back in the day was that he showed me a lot of attention. He was driving when we met, and he had access to his family cars, and we didn't have to catch a bus. He would pick me up from school and take me other places I wanted to go. He was a good listener. After being with him for a couple of months, I started talking to him about me being an adoptee. He would always listen and seem to understand me with showing me much compassion. After we had been together for about one year, I became pregnant, and we got married. I had a connection with someone, my friend, who later became my husband. When my son was born, this was a part of me and the same with my daughter when she was born, I have a family that belongs to me, and bloodline connects us. I loved them, and they showed love back to me. My family made me feel good as being a wife and a mother, but there was still something that wasn't complete. I would love to have had more children, but after our marriage became rocky, I decided it was best that we didn't.

After many trials our marriage went through, Freddy would always come back and apologize to me, and we would try again to make our marriage work. It was many times that I thought to leave him; but I didn't want to break that family connection, not really realizing that it was already broken and one person cannot put the pieces together. We were married for 26 years until Freddy filed for a divorce and I was served with divorce papers. It was a devastating time for me. I had just had surgery and was recovering and on medical leave. I felt rejected, hurt, in pain, abandoned, lost and again, the feeling of being a castaway resurfaced. Not to be wanted anymore by him caused the feeling of having a friend, husband, lover, soul mate, and confidant to end. After he filed for the divorce, I began to hate and despise him. I had to keep praying, asking God to help me through this and to help me with forgiveness.

I went to a support group program that my job, the Salvation Army's Director, had told me about. My church sponsored me to go. It was the best thing for me. I recommend it to anyone who is going through a divorce to attend the workshops. It was "Divorce Recovery Workshops" with a study guide and book, by Jim Smoke called "Growing through Divorce." It was an eight weeks' program, where we met once a week at the Ward Presbyterian Church in Northville, Michigan. It was sponsored by their Single Point Ministries. It helped me very much in adjusting to a very difficult situation. Going through the program helped me to release something out of my life. It also helped me, knowing who I am and being adopted, using some of the same principles. Knowing that you will never be completely healed until you forgive. I started to recover and heal from the divorce.

Freddy had married for a second and third time, but each one of the marriages didn't work out and ended up in divorce. Time went on, and because of my going through the Divorce Recovery Workshops God gave back to me His love for Freddy, and we became good friends. In 2012, when I was reunited with my biological father and met my four brothers, Freddy was with me, and he helped me through it. He was happy for me and reminded me that my prayers had been answered.

On Sunday morning, November 1, 2015, I lost my friend Freddy died from the result of a car accident.

For in him we live, and move, and have our being; Acts 17:28

This is what I have found to be true. It is in God that I live. I have the feeling now of being complete, and I know it is from God. Now that I have found myself, my destiny is to help other adoptees to know who they are, even if they don't know their biological parents.

Being Made Whole

The two different halves of my life have made me a whole person today. Because of my birth mother carrying me in her womb for nine months, I am here on this earth. We only had a short time together, but she gave me life. She nurtured and took care of me while in the womb, and I believe she had good prenatal care. I was told that when I was born, I was a healthy baby who weighted 7lbs., 2 ½ oz. and 20 inches long. I am grateful for her birthing me into this world and not aborting me. So many different things could have happened, while she was carrying me, but they didn't. I heard that when some young girls got pregnant back in the day, some tried to do all kind of things to their bodies trying to abort their babies and because of the harm, some babies were born with defects in their bodies of what the mothers tried to do. I don't know how my birth mother felt after I was born, but I don't think she had a chance to look at me before we were separated and went into different directions. I still would like to talk with my birth mother about this. After I found her, it was a joy for me, and I was content. I would love to have a closer relationship with my birth mother and sister, but I respect their wishes. The last time I saw her was when I went to visit her in 1989. I talked with her over the phone several times, but they were brief conversations. Because of the love of God that is within me, I have love for my birth mother and sister. I don't hold anything against her for giving me up for adoption. She was a desperate young girl, that knew she couldn't give me the life she wanted me to have, but she gave me a chance to live. When her pregnancy happened, she chose to deal with it.

My biological mother graduated from high school and enrolled in a junior college. In 1960, she had another child, which was a girl. After that child, she did not have any more children. She married a man from Detroit, and the family later moved out of state. She further her education and earn a bachelor degree. She is now retired, and she and her husband have been married for over 50 years.

My biological father graduated from high school and later got married. He and his wife begin to start a family. He enlisted in the U.S. Army and served for two years. He is a hard worker and a man that provided well for his family. He retired in 2002. He and his wife have four sons and have been married for over 55 years.

The other half is my adoptive parents who invested their lives in me. I lived with them for almost 17 years. As I mentioned before, my adoptive parents gave me the best of things, which only are temporary, but the one thing they gave me and taught me, that will affect me for a lifetime, is to know how to pray and to know the Lord.

I thank God; I am a blessed child. I know God has His hands on me. I never experienced any physical, mental or sexual abuse. I did get a couple of whippings, but I can count how many of them it was on my hand. I was raised in a loving, God-fearing home.

When growing up, the greatest fear wasn't so much of my being adopted and given up by my birth mother to strangers, but it was that I was raised as an only child. I think if I had a brother or sister to grow up with me, maybe I wouldn't have thought so much about my adoption. I guess! Another thing about adoption that keeps us guessing and wondering, you will never know how it would have been with living with your birth parents and knowing them.

I had a wonderful life and was raised as a princess. I had two moms that wanted the best for me, and because of my life, I am now made whole and complete.

My mother and father-in-law (in-love) also have poured into my life. They have been parents to me. Even when Freddy and I had divorced, they didn't divorce me. They always supported me, gave me good advice, and showed love for my children and me. When I found my biological families, they always told me, no matter what happens they would be there for me, and they were praying for me. It means a lot when you know someone has your back and no matter what will support you. It is time now, as I am writing this book that our family has to show them support. Shortly, after

Freddy died, my mother-in-law grieved over his death, and she suffered two strokes and was in and out of the hospital, until April 2016, when she went into a nursing home. My father-in-law did really well. He went to see her every day and helps to feed her. On December 17, 2016 the Lord called my mother-in-law from labor to reward. She had suffered long enough. She was 87 years old. My In-laws had been married for 66 years, and if the Lord allows my father-in-law to live to make it to November 29, 2017, he will be 90 years old.

While writing this book, I went through some ups and downs, but God sees to it that I am always overcoming. There's been some good times and not so good, but I am always thankful for spending time with my family. My grandson did graduate from high school and is a freshman at Western Michigan University, in Kalamazoo, Michigan, majoring in Mechanical Engineering.

I had a corneal transplant on my right eye on June 27, 2016. I had learned some years ago, that I have an eye disorder called Keratoconus. When the doctor told me I had this disorder, of course, I thought about my biological family. Did I get this from them?

Keratoconus is a slowly progressive condition often presenting in the teens or early twenties with decreased vision or visual distortion. This condition is typically not associated with redness, inflammation or other "acute" symptoms and therefore may go undetected for long periods of time. Over 90% of patients have involvement of both eyes, though it is not unusual for there to be asymmetric changes with one eye being more involved than the other. In most cases, the cornea is the only part of the eye that is abnormal. The doctor stated a family history of keratoconus is occasionally seen. I tried to wear glasses for a period of time, and the cornea steepens and became more irregular to the glasses. I went to wearing hard or gas permeable contact lenses for around 15 years. I had a lot of trouble wearing the contacts. So, this year is when the doctor told me the best thing would be to have that transplant. I can see a little better, but I still need surgery in my right eye for a cataract.

I am so glad that I now know my purpose and the destiny God has for me. Because I am destined to succeed, there is still more fulfillment in me toward my destiny.

"This is not a time to get distracted,
This is not a time to go off course,
This is not a time to lose your focus
Got a work to do for the Lord
And you cannot afford to lose your way
You've come too far from where you started
So please don't let the time you've sown be wasted
On things that you'll later regret
Wishing you never had
Once you realize it wasn't worth it
Your destiny is too important to give up for anything."

This is another song that I love, by Kevin LeVar – *"Your Destiny."*

Fulfill Your Destiny

To all adoptive mothers who have adopted children, please tell them, when they are a young age that they are adopted. If you don't tell them, somebody else will. Let them know that "adoption was a decision the adults made and that you love them and you are a family." Emphasize that your child had nothing to do with the decision and more importantly, did nothing to create the situation.

To the birth mothers who have kept secrets about the child you gave up for adoption, please let your immediate family know that you had a child and it was given up for adoption. You don't know when that child will come searching for you. You can believe that the child you gave up, often thinks about their birth mother and father.

Adoption is a lifelong process, either you love it or hate it, but it's for life.

Epilogue

My Steps Are Ordered
The Lord directs the steps of the Godly. He delights in every detail of their lives.
Psalms 37:23 NLT

It's not by accident or coincident but by the divine order of God. Throughout this journey, God has truly ordered my steps!

I mentioned before how I grew up on the east side of Detroit, and my biological parents grew up in the same neighborhood. If my adoptive parents had stayed in the same neighborhood, I would have attended the same high school my biological parents graduated from. By us living in the same neighborhood for many years, I believe our paths have crossed, but it wasn't the right time for me to find them.

Even though at times I have gotten off course and got into self, He directed me back on course and told me to keep it moving. This is why I praise him today. **Sometimes the smallest step in the right direction ends up being the biggest step of your life.**

As I look back on my journey as a child, I didn't think too much about being adopted. I felt secure and comfortable and knew my adoptive parents were going to take care of me. It is when I grew into my adolescent years that the questions started coming into my mind. The older I was and the more responsibilities I had, especially as a mother, I wanted to know about my biological family.

The year of 1973, I graduated from high school, and I started my first job, as a secretary, at the Joseph Campau Church of God where I grew up. I worked there from 1973-1976. After I found my biological father, I found out that my paternal grandparents lived four blocks from the church, between the same two streets and had been living there for over 50 years. My paternal grandfather died on July 11, 2011, and my paternal grandmother died on March 4, 2002. I'm glad I had a chance to meet both of them.

After my daughter was one-year-old, I went back to work in 1977, and I had many different jobs from 1977 to 1988. The summer of 1984, is when I went to Children's Aid Society to see if I could get some more information about my biological parents. I still wasn't able to get their names, but I did receive a little more information than what I previously had. I kept walking in the steps that were ordered for me.

Also, in 1988, I became a member of another church, where I talked with a young lady who worked at the high school where my biological parents had attended. She was the one that was instrumental in giving me that important information that led me to find my biological mother, a half-sister, aunts, uncles, and cousins. Later to find my biological father, his wife and my father's parents. At the time of finding them, our relationships didn't turn out as I thought, but at least my questions have been answered. I really didn't know what to expect, but to expect the unexpected? At first, it was like a wall between us and I could only go so far. I left both relationships alone and did not try to pursue them, knowing that God did not let me find them for no reason. For many years, I kept it moving.

The year was 1994 when I went to work at the Salvation Army Denby Center and worked there until 2000. I believed I was placed there to worked with the teenage girls, who were staying there during their pregnancy. It was for me to get a feel of how my biological mother had felt when she was placed in a home when she was pregnant with me.

When I left the Salvation Army Denby Center in the year 2000, for a better job at the L.I.F.T. Center and I worked there until 2011. All the brokenness I went through, I was able to mend, build up, and establish my self-sufficiency and self-worth. When the job ended at L.I.F.T., I was very disappointed, because my plan was to retire from L.I.F.T. But God took what the enemy meant for evil, and He turned it for my good.

In January of 2005, I was looking for a new church home. I had made a list of churches I was planning to visit. Greater Grace Temple was not on my list. I went to Greater Grace that particular Sunday because it was cold and there was quite a bit of snow. I was used to going to church every Sunday, so I thought since Greater Grace is just a few blocks away from my home, I would go there. From that Sunday on, I didn't visit any other churches but became a member in June 2005. The place that was once Edgewater Amusement Park where I was hurt, from seeing my husband with another woman, has now become the healing place in my life, which is Greater Grace Temple Church.

In our new member's class, I met Deborah Starr-Hodges, and we became good friends. When she found out that L.I.F.T. had terminated the employees in 2011, Deborah was instrumental in me becoming employed at Capuchin's Soup Kitchen. It was at Capuchin's Service Center that I found my biological brother. The wall on my paternal side of the family has been torn down, and we are building on our relationships with one another.

It was just like Ecclesiastes 3:1-8 KJV says:

1. *To every thing there is a season, and a time to every purpose under the heaven:*
2. *A time to be born, and a time to die, a time to plant, and it time to pluck up that which is planted;*
3. *A time to kill, and a time to heal, a time to break down, and a time to build up*
4. *A time to weep, and a time to laugh, a time to mourn, and a time to dance:*
5. *A time to cast away stones, and a time to gather stones together, a time to embrace, and a time to refrain from embracing;*
6. *A time to get, and a time to lose, a time to keep, and a time to cast away.*
7. *A time to rend, and a time to sew, a time to keep silence, and a time to speak;*
8. *A time to love, and a time to hate, a time of war, and a time of peace.*

Everything in my life happened at the time God ordained. Sometimes, I had to tiptoe in taking a step, but always looking for something positive in each one.

The Paradox

Adoption is…
a concept, a belief and an action
A lack of choice and being chosen
A legal solution to a spiritual problem
A spiritual solution to a legal problem
A loving choice and a thrusting upon
A nurturing touch yet a stealing away

It saved me; yet damaged me
Provided for me, yet took away from me
Blessed me yet cursed me
Gave me a name and took a name
It creates a chance for love to grow and a door for misunderstanding
It creates a family out of strangers and strangers out of family
It inspires and teaches and it wounds and damages

Adoption is…
My friend and my enemy
A thorn in my side and my shining light
A rainbow and a gravestone
Acceptance and rejection
Truth and lies
Known and unknown
Love and hatred
A casting away and returning

Adoption is…
Not the excuse or the cause
Not perfect or evil
Not the reason or the scapegoat
Not who I am or who I am not
Everything and nothing

by Lynn Grubb
Used by permission.

If you're on a journey seeking answers to questions you have inside, remember that God understands. There is an ordained time for every step in the process. The Bible tells us in Ephesians 1:4-6 that God is our adoptive parent.

> *⁴ According as he hath chosen us in him before the foundation of the world, that we should be holy and without blame before him in love:*
>
> *⁵ Having predestinated us unto the adoption of children by Jesus Christ to himself, according to the good pleasure of his will,*
>
> *⁶ To the praise of the glory of his grace, wherein he hath made us accepted in the beloved.*

Trust Him to lead you. No matter where the journey takes you He is already there.

Bibliography

Chapter One: Take A Look Inside

"Know, Learn & Share the FACTS about Life." *Prolife Across America.* Prolife Across America, Web. 19 Apr. 2017. <http://prolifeacrossamerica.org/baby-developmental-facts/?gclid>.

"Week by Week Pregnancy." *HealthyWomen.org.* Healthy Women, Web. 19 Apr. 2017. <http://www.healthywomen.org/category/tags/week-week-pregnancy>.

GotQuestions.org. "Does the Bible Teach That Life Begins at Conception?" *GotQuestions.org.* 15 May 2017. Web. 16 Sept. 2017. <https://gotquestions.org/life-begin-conception.html>.

"When Does Life Begin." *When Does Life Begin: Just The Facts.* Web. 19 Apr. 2017. <http://www.justthefacts.org/get-the-facts/when-life-begins/>.

Adoptions, Inc. American. "American Adoptions -- America's Adoption Agency." *Abortion or Adoption - Know the Facts Before Deciding.* Web. 19 Apr. 2017. <http://www.americanadoptions.com/pregnant/deciding_between_abortion_or_adoption>.

Chapter Two: Disconnected

"What Is the Umbilical Cord? - Health Questions." *NHS Choices.* NHS, Web. 19 Apr. 2017. <http://www.nhs.uk/chq/Pages/2299.aspx>.

Services, Michigan Department Of Human. *DHS-Pub-823: Michigan.gov.* Michigan Department of Human Services. Web. 19 Apr. 2017. <http://www.michigan.gov/documents/dhs/DHS-PUB-0823_221566_7.pdf>.

Hamner, Tommie J., and Pauline H. Turner. *Parenting in Contemporary Society.* Boston, MA: Allyn and Bacon, 2001. Print.

Murray, Rheana. "Woman, 92, Adopts 76-year-old Daughter." *TODAY.com*. TODAY, 10 June 2015. Web. 19 Apr. 2017. <https://www.today.com/parents/texas-mom-muriel-clayton-92-adopts-daughter-mary-smith-76-t25561>.

Chapter Three: Chosen

"Home." *About MARE*. Judson Center, Web. 19 Apr. 2017. <http://www.mare.org/Resources/About-MARE>.

Build A Bear. "About Us Build-A-Bear." *Build-A-Bear Workshop*. Web. 19 Apr. 2017. <http://www.buildabear.com/about-us/>.

Rhoads, Denise. "Storytelling Research Projects by SLIS 5440 Students." *The Popularity of Teddy Bears in Stories - Denise Rhoads*. University of North Texas, Web. 19 Apr. 2017. <https://courses.unt.edu/efiga/STORYTELLING/Rhoads_Project.htm>.

Southey, Robert. "Lit2Go." *"The Three Bears" | Fairy Tales and Other Traditional Stories | Robert Southey | Lit2Go ETC*. Web. 25 Sept. 2017. <http://etc.usf.edu/lit2go/68/fairy-tales-and-other-traditional-stories/5105/the-three-bears/>.

Chapter Five: The Question Is?

"June." *June - Baby Girl Name Meaning and Origin | Oh Baby! Names*. Oh Baby! Names, Web. 19 Apr. 2017. <http://www.ohbabynames.com/meaning/name/june/848#.Wb1XfrKGMdU>.

Hackett, Julie. "The Power Behind a Name." *The Power Behind a Name: Martin Luther King, Jr. - Baby News - Oh Baby! Names*. Oh Baby! Names, Web. 19 Apr. 2017. <http://www.ohbabynames.com/baby-news/the-power-behind-a-name-martin-luther-king-jr/57#.Wb1ZcbKGMdU>.

Chapter Six: Help! I'm Trying to Find Myself

Warren, Richard. *The Purpose-driven Life: What on Earth Am I Here For?* Grand Rapids, MI: Zondervan, 2002. Print.

Talcott, Kimberly. "A Question of Motherhood." *Guideposts Magazine* Sept. 2015: 46. Print. Volume 70 Issue 7

"Pernicious Anemia: MedlinePlus Medical Encyclopedia." *U.S. National Library of Medicine*. National Institutes of Health, Web. 19 Apr. 2017. <http://www.nlm.nih.gov/medlineplus/ency/article/000569.htm>.

Healing Thoughts. Unity, 2005. Print.

Chapter Nine: Connected by Grace

Owens, Rudy. "Posts about Florence Crittenton Homes on Rudy Owens' Blog." *Rudy Owens' Blog*. Web. 15 Sept. 2017. <https://rudyowensblog.com/tag/florence-crittenton-homes/>.

Chapter Eleven: Complete in Him

Kevin LeVar – "Your Destiny."

Keratoconus – Michigan Cornea Consultants – Patient Education Series - Steven P. Dunn, M.D., David G. Heidemann, M.D. & Christopher Y.C. Chow, M.D.

Epilogue

Grubb, Lynn. "Search Results for The+Paradox," *Adoption Education & Resources*. Lynn Grubb, 01 Jan. 1970. Web. 7 Jan. 2017. http://noapologiesfobeingme.blogspot.com/search?q=the%2Bparadox>

About the Author

June Purifoy is a people-oriented and enthusiastic woman committed to Human Services.

Presently she works as an Emergency Assistance Intake Worker for the Capuchin Soup Kitchen's Service Center, a ministry within the Province of St. Joseph of the Capuchin Order. She has been blessed to have the opportunity to provide resources and emotional support to others working with other non-profit organizations as well.

June has worked with pregnant teen moms, as well as women in substance abuse, domestic violence, and homeless shelters. These experiences led to obtaining an Associate's Degree in Family Life Education from Great Lakes Christian College, Certificate in School of Management from the Institute of Black Family Development and a Certificate in Case Management from Wayne County Community College.

June has served as president of the Women's Ministry of the Greenfield Church of God for 11 years and established women to believe in themselves and to build up their self-esteem and self-worth, with workshops, seminars, and the affirmation of "I Promise Myself."

God has blessed June in the last couple of years to be united with her biological father and four brothers. After her search to find her biological families, June has found herself. Because of God, she knows the purpose for her life.

June is a member of the Greater Grace Temple Church under the leadership of Bishop Charles H. Ellis. She is a member of the Powerful Women of Purpose and the Metro Detroit Scribes for Christ.

June is single, a mother of two adult children and grandmother of three.

www.ingramcontent.com/pod-product-compliance
Lightning Source LLC
Chambersburg PA
CBHW071630080526
44588CB00010B/1341